Living Low Sodium

Living Low Sodium

A guide for understanding our relationship with sodium and how to be successful in adhering to a low-sodium diet

Mark Knoblauch, PhD

Kiremma Press
Houston, TX

www.authorMK.com

ISBN: 978-1-7320674-4-8

No matter your reason for engaging in a low-sodium diet, no matter whether the undertaking is for you or a loved one, this book is written for and dedicated to you, for I too have been through the challenges and frustrations that you will experience every day

Table of Contents

Preface

If you're reading this book you no doubt are either interested in a low-sodium lifestyle, are already in a low-sodium lifestyle, or you are associated with someone who is. If the first two aspects relate to you then you've probably already done some research on the topic, or perhaps you've learned of the difficulties that a low-sodium diet can entail. If the latter applies and you are associated with someone – such as a spouse, child, or parent – who is engaged in a low-sodium diet, then you have my respect for making the effort to learn more about adhering to this particular type of lifestyle.

I use the word 'lifestyle' for a reason, for when it comes to low-sodium and the many different aspects and challenges involved, you will find that it's not as much of a diet as it is a complete lifestyle adjustment. The low-sodium lifestyle is not necessarily easy nor is it for everyone, but it can bring a wealth of benefits as we will discuss at length in this book. Yet at the same time going low-sodium can also bring stress, frustration, and a significant amount of extra effort. But just by reading this book and attempting to become more educated about the lifestyle, you are gaining yourself a great start.

There are so many diets out there. Gluten-free, low-carb, Keto, and a wealth of others. Many of these diets tout health-related benefits, while others focus on weight loss as a known benefit. A low-sodium diet is not really designed for weight loss as much as it is for improvement of several health-related aspects such as blood pressure, maintaining body fluid levels, etc. As such, going low-sodium is more designed for health improvement than weight loss. Yes, you might lose some weight, but it is tough to directly state that the weight loss results from decreasing your overall sodium intake as much as from eating healthier foods that most likely also contain less sodium. Still, if undertaking a low-sodium diet there is certainly a good chance that you will lose at least some weight; however, the bigger expectation is that you will make some important health improvements. Therefore, regardless of whether you were told to go on a low-sodium diet or if you just want to take on the challenge in order to improve your health, your efforts are to be commended.

So what is this book about? Clearly, its main focus centers around the low-sodium diet. But what does that entail? To answer that question, let me first tell you what this book is *not* about. It's not a book designed to sell you anything. So many diet and health books on the market that set out little teasers for you, only to later reveal that you will need to sign up for some website in order to get the important material. I have seen that happen too many times, so this book, like all my books, is designed to both teach you and help you help yourself by providing you a wealth of material on the topic that you can then use to learn more about, and improve, your own life. Personally, I have nothing to sell you and no product to recommend – other than this book itself. Therefore, this book is designed to *teach* rather than *sell.* Secondly, this book is not a recipe book. I want to provide you the foundation to understand *why* sodium influences our health. I have spent my life as an educator, and one of my long-held beliefs is that students learn better when they understand foundational concepts that they can then use as a basis for understanding any new material on the topic. Therefore, instead of just throwing a bunch of facts at you, I would prefer to teach you the "why" and "how" of various aspects of sodium and its effects on our body.

So then, what exactly is this book about now that you know what it's *not* about? Well, as I just stated, this book is designed to teach you the basics of sodium specific to how it affects your body and how lowering your sodium can play a role in improving your health. In learning the basics, you can in turn decide for yourself if adhering to a low-sodium diet is for you. Even if you feel that you aren't going to benefit much from a low-sodium diet, I hope that in reading this book you feel you are more knowledgeable on the topic of sodium and how it affects your body. To help you learn more, we'll start off with an introduction of my own journey with sodium, followed by a brief look into the historical use of sodium both in industry as well as in how our consumption of sodium has changed over time. We'll then take a look at sodium's scientific characteristics such as its role as an atom and an ion, both of which play a major role in your body.

Next we'll examine in more detail how sodium affects your body, including how sodium can *negatively* affect your body by triggering certain medical conditions. Then we'll explore how sodium has become such a predominant factor in our life by discussing sodium's role in the food industry including its role as a seasoning and as a preservative. Finally, we'll close out the book by discussing how you can better monitor your sodium level, particularly in learning how to understand and interpret a nutrition label.

I hope that you find this book to be a comprehensive guide to help you on your own low-sodium journey. Without a doubt, going and staying low-sodium can be a long and arduous journey. I know because I've been there and I have every intent of staying there! In my own journey with this lifestyle I've had many learning opportunities and even a few hiccups along the way. My intent with this book is to provide you a reference that can help you be successful on your own journey, perhaps even helping you avoid your own hiccups as well.

One final note before we begin. This book is not designed to tell you that you must go on a low-sodium diet; rather, that should be a decision that you either make on your own or through consultation with your medical professional. I have had tremendous success staying low-sodium, but you may have more or less success in your own journey. Because a low-sodium diet can be a shock to your system, no matter your reason for starting such a diet, it's always recommended that you discuss your intentions with your medical professional. And, take on the low-sodium diet slowly in order to allow your body time to adapt. It's hoped that over time you will find your own benefits of going low-sodium. But, this diet and this lifestyle is not for everyone. Therefore, be honest with yourself, adhere to the advice of your medical professional, and if you're going to try it, give it an honest shot.

With that being said, let's get started in tackling the rationale behind low-sodium diets and get you on a path to better health!

Chapter 1. About me

My guess is that by this point in your journey to learn more about going low-sodium you have recognized that there are quite a few books on the market that discuss the benefits of reducing your sodium intake. Believe me, I know. I too looked for some kind of guide to help get me started on my low sodium journey. What I found was that a lot of the same concepts were presented over and over in slightly different packages. So many books tout a low-sodium diet, but they all emphasized recipes rather than teaching the reader anything. I found very little information about navigating the low-sodium lifestyle and nothing specific to *what is happening in my body*. There was nothing to explain *why* I was having the problems I was having other than a sweeping generalization that high-sodium diets can be problematic. This lack of a basic background about sodium and its effects in the human body is what ultimately drove me to look into writing my own book.

When I first envisioned this book, my intent was to provide a resource for those individuals on low-sodium diets by focusing on the science of sodium and its effects in the body, as well as providing a practical guide that will help consumers make smarter decisions regarding the sodium content of the foods they eat. Ultimately, I hope that you will find that I have followed through on that goal. But as I approached the finish line of writing my initial draft of this book, I realized that you the reader won't have an opportunity to understand who I am, nor will you know my own qualifications for bringing you this book. So I reassessed the design of the book and determined that I should open with a chapter introducing myself and also outlining for you the struggles and the accomplishments that I have had in adjusting to a low sodium diet. In doing so, I think that it will help you the reader understand that I too am familiar with the frustrations and inconveniences that adhering to a low-sodium diet can bring.

Let the dizziness begin

Throughout most of my life I have been lucky enough to have progressed relatively injury-free. Other than a couple of broken bones associated with physical activity, I had zero experience with hospitals throughout my first 35 years. This all changed toward the end of 2009. I was a full-time student in the fourth year of my doctorate work, surviving on a small teaching stipend while working at times four part-time jobs in order to make ends meet. As a student and a former practicing clinician in the medical field, I'd long had an interest in muscles and how they respond to physical activity, especially the seemingly odd fact that the harder you work a muscle, the stronger it becomes. I had spent the first few years of my graduate classes learning about ions, cell signaling, membrane channels, and pumps, as all were involved in my research that centered around an event termed "skeletal muscle damage" –

a fancy term for the events that cause the soreness you feel for the next couple of days after strenuous activity.

One early Monday morning at around 3 a.m. (I still remember my first few dizzying events *very* clearly) I woke up in a sweat, effectively unable to see anything due to the fact that my eyes were rapidly shooting back and forth uncontrollably. As I sat up in bed I had a fit of intense vertigo that forced me to immediately lay back down, followed by a sudden surge of nausea. As I tried to stand up I was immediately and rapidly forced to the ground by the vertigo. Eventually I was able to muster the effort to crawl to the toilet, followed shortly thereafter by the most physically strenuous vomiting I have ever experienced. Vomiting so powerful that it made my shoulder and neck muscles hurt for two days afterwards. Five minutes after the vomiting ended I was able to crawl back to bed, where laying as still as possible was the only remedy I could find as the vertigo continued.

Eventually I fell back to sleep. Waking up, I realized that the nausea and vertigo were gone. At first I thought the misery had run its course, but I now had a strange sensation that felt as if I had just finished spinning in a circle. Not the spinning part itself, but rather the immediate after-effects. Then, once I was able to get dressed and venture outside my apartment, I noticed a strange 'haze' that made it seem as though everything was brighter – to the point I had to squint anytime I was in sunlight or a well-lit area.

Throughout the day I noticed the onset of a new event, one that made it seem as though my eyes suddenly didn't work right. If I stared at a very small point – such as a period on this page – for just a few seconds, my eyes would quickly jump to

19

the side. This effect became more noticeable over the next few days to the point that my vision would "shake" as my eyes made constant, tiny uncontrolled movements. I could still read fine and function normally, but concentrating on a small object became problematic.

Though I hadn't paid much attention to it, I had for the previous year or so been having issues with my right ear. A constant 'howling' sound prevailed, as if I had a seashell perpetually held up against it. Now, after this severe vertigo bout I noticed that certain 'everyday' sounds became louder. Getting pots out of a cabinet or any other sudden sounds (clapping, hammering, etc.) actually *hurt*, something that prior to my dizziness attack I didn't even know was physically possible.

Although I never figured out what caused that first attack, I was soon offered many more opportunities. Along with the onset of these new sensations, I began experiencing several more attacks over the next few weeks. These attacks involved severe vertigo, profuse full-body sweating, and eventually a staggered crawl to the bathroom for a round of forceful vomiting. Once my dry-heaving was done I felt a general desire to lay still in bed for the remainder of the attack, which would typically last from 3 to 4 hours. Once the end of the attack approached, I would feel an overwhelming urge to sleep. This urge was not something I could fight through as I often wanted to (due to pending work or home responsibilities). So the only option was to give in and sleep, knowing that upon waking up an hour or two later I would generally be back to normal, or at least to the point that I could function adequately.

Sometimes the vertigo would present itself as a full-on attack. Other times I would experience what I called a 'blip' that would start out with the seeming intent of an attack but quickly dissipate to just a sort of 'warning shot'. As one might imagine, the unpredictability of being stuck for 3-4 hours in a bout of severe vertigo caused quite a bit of anxiety for me as well. This anxiety became so bad and so controlling that for the first time in my life I talked to my doctor about going on medication – alprazolam – to help me deal with the anxiety caused by this strange condition that I did not understand nor have any way to control.

In my fit to find some degree of explanation for what I was experiencing, I began reading about panic attacks, psychological disorders, stroke, heart conditions, and a wealth of other events that I could somehow rationalize into being a potential cause for my condition. Nothing seemed to be working. Because of the anxiety brought on by the thought of experiencing an unexpected attack, I began to avoid social situations, driving, and in some cases even avoiding the chance of being a passenger for fear of the vehicle's turning and braking sensations actually triggering an attack. By mid-2011 I had seemingly run the course of medical specialists – my personal physician, an ear, nose, and throat physician, a cardiologist, and even a neurologist. Every time the answer was the same: *your test results are fine, so just try to 'relax'.*

To this day I don't know if it's more frustrating or reassuring to be told by medical professionals that there's nothing wrong with you. On the one hand you feel relief that you're not dying but yet on the other hand you're no closer to solving the initial problem. And hearing the same response

21

over and over from physicians wears your spirit down quickly. Particularly frustrating was that I knew that the completely debilitating effects of the attacks could not possibly be all in my head, and if only the attacks would happen while I was at a medical professional's office they could see firsthand the profuse sweating, rapid eye movements, inability to stand, and forceful vomiting, and realize that no healthy human has the ability to auto-trigger those events. Something had to be going on, but no one seemed able or qualified to tell me.

Finally, in the fall of 2011 I was completing an internship just down the road from where I had recently received my graduate degree. One night I was invited by my doctoral advisor to attend a social gathering with some of my graduate school professors, and as it was just down the street from where I worked, I was happy to join in. While at the party I happened to sit next to a professor who had done some balance and coordination research on astronauts. In discussing some of the frustrating events I had been having, he outlined a few potential causes of my symptoms. His suggestion was for me to see an ear specialist due to the balance and vertigo issues. In November 2011, without hesitation I took his advice and saw an otoneurologist who happened to practice in the same medical center where I was completing my internship. There, upon hearing my symptoms about the attacks in addition to the vision and hearing issues, tests were ordered that eventually confirmed a diagnosis of Ménière's disease.

Ménière's disease is a somewhat poorly understood condition. It is believed that the disorder results when fluid levels within the inner ear are not able to be maintained properly. When this occurs, the body's ability to detect motion and movement are thrown off, which in turn causes the patient to experience Ménière's-associated symptoms such as vertigo, nausea, etc. There is no known cause of Ménière's, though it most often occurs somewhat spontaneously in an older (>60 years) population. I learned during my initial diagnosis that there is no cure, but many options exist for Ménière's treatment which include the avoidance of caffeine and limiting one's salt intake in order to help prevent the fluid buildup within the ear. I happily took that dietary advice – along with a prescription for some medication to help excrete additional salt from my body – and went on my way.

For the next few months I felt pretty good. I avoided salt – or so I thought – by not eating fast foods, soups, or other traditionally high-salt foods. The nystagmus (i.e. shaky vision) remained, but the attacks stopped and for the most part I was feeling pretty good about the situation. Perhaps I became a bit too confident over time, as the absence of attacks led me to believe that my approach was working successfully and perhaps I could 'cheat' a little. One Sunday night about six months after my diagnosis I made a pot roast in the crock pot. Giving no thought to the potential danger, I added an onion soup packet to the crock pot for a little additional flavoring. Without a constant reminder of my symptoms I never once thought to check the salt or sodium content of the pack. Perhaps this one little opportunity for flavoring would be OK, right?

Unfortunately I was wrong – more wrong than ever before when it came to my food choices. Initially, I had a few issues with imbalance the next two days that I thought would quickly pass. But then, a couple days after eating the pot roast,

I was walking to lunch in the middle of a major medical center when I stepped off a curb to cross the street. The instant my foot hit the concrete a powerful vertigo attack hit me right there in the middle of an intersection. I was laid out on the ground with two cars now idling at the stop sign five feet away, and people were suddenly flocking around me. While trying to get my bearings I was telling these people I was fine, just asking them to let me be. A minute later I was able to walk on my own as the initial balance loss had subsided, but my mission now turned towards finding a quiet room before the attack got more severe, so as to let the attack run its course over the next couple hours. I still clearly remember sitting in that dark room I found, the tapping sound of my sweat dripping off my chin and hitting a paper sack in the trash can below me. It was almost as if it was a sort of warning to indicate the violence of the attack that was approaching. It was to date my most severe attack, and one that I will never forget.

The next day I was back at the otoneurologist's office. This time, I was both desperate and desolate. I was now willing to do anything to fix the problem I was having, as I couldn't afford another attack like the one I'd had the previous day. My wife and I were expecting my first child in two weeks, yet I was oblivious to that event given the severity of the recent attack. All I could think about was that there was no way I was going to live out my next 40 years with the randomness of a completely debilitating disorder holding me hostage, all while trying to raise a family. What I will say is that I was at the lowest point in my life during this time, despite my heart telling me that I should have been preparing to be at my highest with the impending birth of my daughter.

At the physician's office, I told the physician that I had cut my salt intake a good deal since my initial visit with him. I made it clear that I had stopped adding salt. I'd been avoiding soups and fast food and other high-sodium items. He then started asking me more specific questions about my diet, and we began to analyze my food choices. For example, when I said that I had been eating a lot of salads, he asked about my salad dressing and how much dressing I use. I naively replied that I would put about half a cup on, which he pointed out (and I was later embarrassed to learn) was contributing an extremely high amount of sodium to my diet. We continued our conversation with him explaining hidden sodium in foods, and I became somewhat inspired as his advice made me realize that making smarter sodium-based food choices had a real chance of helping me continue to recover.

After I left his office, I was on a mission to cut sodium out of my diet. I was motivated to build off the small successes I'd had after my initial visit six months earlier, and began to think that a more religious adherence to a low sodium diet might further improve my symptoms. Over the next few days my pantry received an overhaul, my lunches became much healthier, and I began to read up on how to cut out unnecessary sodium. Though it took a few weeks to start feeling normal again – even through the birth of my daughter – over time I began to notice a further decrease in my symptoms. Two months later, I was – by my own impressions – fully recovered. The attacks did not return, the shaky vision and ear howling were gone, and the constant dizziness that I had grown accustomed to had disappeared. I was shocked as much as I was thrilled. And I knew that I was going to do whatever I needed to do to prevent a return to what I had just gone through with Ménière's.

Reinventing a lifestyle

Prior to my diagnosis with Ménière's I had no real concept of sodium. Granted, I had worked with it in a lab and applied it amply on foods for years; however, I did not *understand* it nor its effects on the body. After my diagnosis, I became almost obsessed with sodium in food, driven by the fact that decreasing my sodium intake had taken me from a literal state of emotional and physical despair to an almost complete return to normal. I eventually stopped taking medication as well. I had already weaned myself off the alprazolam after having been told it would have no effect on the attacks, but I also quit the diuretic and the drug Histamine, which was shown to have positive effects for Ménière's sufferers. I had no further issues driving, turning corners, nor walking down long, straight hallways that had previously triggered anxiety due to making me feel as though I were about to have an attack. Remember, all of these improvements occurred after I made the switch to low sodium. Consequently, my curiosity as a researcher led me to want to understand more about the relationship that our bodies have with sodium. And the more I learned, the more my mind shifted towards wanting to 'beat the system' imposed on us by the food industry specific to sodium.

Eventually, I settled in on about a 1000mg per day diet. This is much lower than the recommended 2300mg diet that the government sets, and vastly lower than the 3400mg or more of sodium that most Americans intake. No matter the inconveniences I may have in adhering to a low sodium diet, there is no amount of sacrificing food convenience, taste, or cost that will risk my going back to a life filled with the symptoms of Ménière's. Won't do it. Not gonna happen.

Staying active on a low sodium diet

Returning to 'normal' after suffering the symptoms of Ménière's can be invigorating. So invigorating that it might drive you to do things you never thought possible, at least not while suffering from Ménière's. I can say that this happened for me, anyway. A year after I made the low-sodium switch I had an urge to kick up my running distances and try a half marathon. Up until then, my furthest competitive distance had been a 5K, and my longest casual run had been seven miles, all of which had occurred several years earlier and prior to the onset of my Ménière's symptoms. But with a new lease on life I had developed a mindset that if Ménière's ever returns in a way that I cannot control – in other words, if it returns even while I'm on a low-sodium diet – I want to have accomplished what I can in the time I can before it returns. So, I set out to run a half-marathon, which I eventually did. Then I ran a couple more just for kicks. In 2015 the urge was strong to push past doing "half" of anything, so I developed the bug to try a full marathon. A few months later, that goal was achieved. Eventually, with several marathons behind me, I thought I had done everything I wanted that was on my Ménière's 'bucket list'.

To understand the significance of these running accomplishments, you have to understand the mindset of endurance athletes and perhaps a bit of the physiology involved in endurance activity. When you exercise, you begin to sweat. When you sweat, you remove sodium from the body. And when your body loses sodium, it is believed that you increase your risk of cramping in addition to reducing your body's performance capacity, among other things. To counter these effects, running competitions stock their food stations with high-sodium items such as pretzels, chips, salt packets, etc. (along with some fruit and electrolyte replacement drinks as well). The thought of avoiding salt and sodium-based products is actually quite taboo in the endurance world. Ironically, these same items were taboo to me as a Ménière's sufferer given that they interfered with my maintaining a low-sodium diet. Consequently, every event I entered put me at odds with what I needed to do – consume sodium – versus what I did not want to do – consume sodium.

The association between sodium loss and exertional activity is well documented. Still, I feared a Ménière's relapse might occur if I consumed too much sodium even during a race, so I continued on with my strict sodium regimen. My attitude during my races was that I'd rather deal with the low-sodium effects (e.g. cramps, reduced muscle force production) than the debilitating effects of a Ménière's attack. Interestingly, the only times I noticed any effects from my low-sodium efforts, it was quite short-lived. The first occurred in early June of 2012 when I went out for a four-mile run a few days after initiating my stringent sodium diet. About three miles in, a sensation started in my chest and literally spread like a wave across my body in every direction. I don't know what it was, but it produced significant exhaustion. I immediately slowed to a walk and eventually the sensation disappeared without a trace, after which I resumed my run. Eventually, this same sensation happened again in early 2016 at mile 18 of my second-ever marathon. Once again, I walked for a bit and the sensation was quickly gone and forgotten. Despite my low sodium intake and exercising in all kinds of weather from cold and windy to hot and humid, to this date these two random events are the only known adverse events that I can tie into my low-sodium lifestyle.

Though I thought the completion of a marathon or two would signal my victory over Ménière's, my mind soon had second-thoughts. In 2015 I volunteered at a half-Ironman event near my home. I had earlier been told by a friend that I should try a triathlon, but my fear was that the rapid head turning associated with the mile-long swim portion of the race would trigger too much dizziness, so I politely declined. However, as I watched people cross the finish line that day while volunteering, I started to wonder if *maybe* I could pull off a half Ironman. it was a step up from a marathon (in my opinion anyway), and it would further prove that I win when it comes to defeating my Ménière's.

I've learned over time that when I wonder if I can do something, it effectively means I'm eventually going to do it. And in April of 2016 that characteristic came true again as I crossed the half-Ironman finish line. I was now content with my newest accomplishment. That is, until I volunteered at the Ironman North American Championships the next month just down the road from my home. What I realized while working at that finish line is that although I felt a true accomplishment and victory over Ménière's by finishing a half-Ironman, I again decided that I would never be content in being a "half" anything (you can't call yourself an 'Ironman' until you finish a full Ironman). So my mind sprang into action again and a couple of months later I signed up for the same Ironman as I had volunteered at. That next April I survived through a 2.4 mile swim, a 112 mile bike, and a marathon. I walked past bins of potato chips, caffeinated drinks, and salt tablets time and time again. I excreted what seemed to be gallons of sodium-filled sweat. And 13 ½ hours after I entered the water for the swim, I became an Ironman. The thrill and accomplishment were great enough that a few months later I signed up for the next one. In 2018 I became a two-time Ironman finisher and took almost 30 minutes off my previous years' time, all while still engaging in a very low-sodium intake during the race. I had taken on Ménière's head on, attempting one of the longest races during which people feel that you need to seemingly be gorging on sodium. My low-sodium challenges against Ménière's were complete, and I felt that I had won each and every challenge I put out.

My point in telling you what I went through with Ménière's is to not only give you a background about me, but also to show you that it *is* possible to function normally when adhering to a low-sodium lifestyle. To be clear, this book is not a book written for Ménière's sufferers; rather, that is just the method by which I began my pathway to becoming low-sodium. Rather, this book is for anyone who wants to partake in a low-sodium lifestyle. You most likely have your own reason(s) designated for why you or someone you know will be going low-sodium, and this book is designed to help you get there. You may have a different medical condition, or just want to improve your health – the reason doesn't matter. What matters is that you are here and that I want to provide you the foundational information that can help you get started on your journey.

Hopefully by telling you my own story it outlines for you that I understand where you're coming from, in that I have my own medically-based reason to maintain a low-sodium diet. These experiences provide me an opportunity to pass on to you what I have learned about the lifestyle over these past seven years. As a scientist and a college professor, I am as interested in learning as I am in teaching, and the intent of this book is to teach you what I have learned about the how and the why of the low-sodium lifestyle. I want to therefore take my own experiences and combine them with my educational background to provide a resource that can help you traverse the low-sodium lifestyle. To do that, in the next chapter we'll look at just what sodium is as an element, which helps set up how our body interacts with sodium for normal function.

Hopefully, when you're finished with this book you will find that no matter the reason for your choosing to embark on a low-sodium lifestyle – whether it be for medical reasons, for improving your health, or because you care about someone else who can benefit from a low-sodium diet – you will find that with just a little bit of effort up front, going low-sodium can be a fun and healthy experience.

Chapter 2 – Sodium Basics

Sodium is one of the most abundant substances on earth. From the vast stretches of the oceans to expansive underground deposits, sodium is all around us. Without it, life as we know it could not exist. Sodium is responsible for our ability to move, breathe, and even think, and is influential for pretty much every living organism around us. As humans, our industrial nature has allowed us to develop ways to take advantage of the physical properties of sodium and use those properties to improve our daily lives. For example, in the food industry we utilize sodium to help our food not only taste better but also stay fresh longer. Despite its wide-reaching presence in our lives, for most of us, sodium is an afterthought that receives little attention beyond a desire to reach for the salt shaker before a meal. Other individuals – such as those adhering to a reduced-sodium diet – often know too well the consequences of excessive sodium intake.

What is it about sodium that makes it so essential for life as we know it but at the same time can have negative consequences for many consumers? The answers to these and many other questions about sodium can be found by first understanding some of the basic properties of sodium. These properties play a key role in how sodium interacts with our physiology, yet when sodium is present in our bodies at excessive levels, these same properties can cause sodium to wreak a degree of havoc on our bodies. In order to fully appreciate how sodium influences our body and our diets we first have to investigate just what it is that makes sodium 'tick'. Therefore, this chapter is designed to introduce you to the basics of sodium. We will first take a brief historical tour to examine how sodium over time became so prominent in our lives. We will then explore where sodium comes from and examine the atomic makeup of sodium, which will help us understand how sodium functions as well as how its structural properties influence its interaction with other substances. Only then can we begin to explore how these fundamental aspects serve as the foundation for the many remarkable processes in which sodium is involved.

A brief history of our relationship with sodium

Few who read this book can argue that when it comes to food, we live in a time of excess. For most of us in the United States, our exposure to and consumption of food is at a level that exceeds any specific dietary needs we may have. Along with a high consumption of food comes all associated ingredients of that food, and sodium is no exception to this. For those of us adhering to a low-sodium diet, the amount of sodium that we consume through easily-accessible sources like fast food and processed food is beyond our tolerable levels and requires careful monitoring to ensure that these levels are not exceeded. But high sodium consumption is no recent trend. As you will see, humans have been consuming very high sodium levels for hundreds of years. Now, however, we are more aware of the consequences of high-sodium diets and can often make positive change when necessary.

Despite being a required nutrient, excess sodium in our diet was not always a concern. In fact, our early ancestors such as *homo erectus* had minimal sodium intake, thought to be limited to that obtained from a primarily meat-based diet [3]. Much of the sodium these ancestors consumed came from eating the meat of grazing animals that subsided on a plant-based diet. The plants supplied sodium to the animals, and consumption of those animals supplied that same sodium (and other nutrients) to early humans. Over time, agricultural advances and population growth spurred an increase in sodium consumption between 5,000 and 10,000 years ago [3]. Further advances in agriculture and food preservation techniques led to what is considered to be the first known use of salt as a preservative by the ancient Egyptians in 2000 BC. Eventually, the influence of salt led to it being considered a valuable commodity that likely contributed to our descendants 1000 years ago consuming approximately five grams (i.e. 5000mg) of salt per day [3]. However, by the 1800s, European communities were consuming a whopping 18 grams of salt (i.e. sodium chloride) per day! Because sodium is 40% of the makeup of sodium chloride, these individuals were consuming almost *eight grams* of sodium per day! By today's recommended sodium intake levels of around 2.3 grams per day, this nearly 350% consumption against todays recommended level may seem quite surprising. But 8 grams actually pales in comparison to what was consumed in northern Europe in the 1500s. Whereas their diets consisted of high amounts of salted fish, it has been estimated that Swedish residents were consuming up to 100 grams of salt *per day* [3]!

Despite a historical trend that indicates an increase in sodium intake over time, our consumption of sodium has decreased dramatically over the past few decades. It is thought that this recent decrease is owed in large part to improvements in food preservation techniques such as refrigeration [3]. Cold storage has all but eliminated the need to preserve meats and other food items in salt or a salt brine as was done historically and which undoubtedly increases the sodium content of those food items. Sodium is still today used extensively to aid in food preservation and is even added to certain food products that are stored frozen, but the sodium levels in those and other foods packaged today do not typically reach the levels used in conjunction with historical food preservation techniques (e.g. curing).

The basics of sodium

I would venture to guess that when you found this book you thought something along the lines of "I hope it will teach me the benefits associated with a low-sodium diet". Without a doubt, that is the overall premise of this book – to help you understand how controlling your sodium intake can help you live a healthy life. I could do that easily in a page or two that lists the known benefits that reducing one's sodium intake can have for many people, but you would really just be reciting facts. I think that understanding concepts would have a much more beneficial result, and in understanding concepts you can then apply what you learn to most any situation. Therefore, to understand the global picture of living a low-sodium lifestyle it is important that you are exposed to the basic properties of sodium as well as how sodium is handled by your body. Similarly, by understanding these basic principles inherent to sodium it should make concepts in future chapters – which outline how your body (Chapter 3) and the food industry (Chapter 5) utilize sodium – more clear as to the role that sodium plays. For example, were I to tell you that drinking seawater actually causes you to be dehydrated, such a concept may be difficult to comprehend given that we are told constantly that staying hydrated is important. But, when you understand that the sudden increase in sodium that your body experiences in response to seawater consumption actually causes fluid to be 'pulled' from your individual cells due to a phenomenon called osmosis, it becomes clear as to why it is important that even when literally dying of thirst, drinking saltwater will serve no benefit and will actually speed up the dying process. Therefore, the rest of this chapter is designed to provide you the foundation for understanding sodium's basic properties in order to lead into our upcoming discussion of how the body handles sodium when it is consumed.

Before we get to the properties of sodium let's take a very brief look at how we came to develop our understanding of sodium. Sodium was first isolated in 1807 when Sir Humphrey Davy was able to extract sodium from the highly caustic substance sodium hydroxide [4]. He noticed during one particular experiment that sodium collected around the negative pole of a battery, and with some precise chemistry and diligent investigation on his part, the discovery of sodium was complete. While we had been reaping the benefits of sodium for thousands of years prior, Davy's experiments allowed us to focus our attempts in on the precise source of those benefits.

Subsequent science and experimentation in the years following Davy's work has led us to what we now know about sodium. As an element, sodium ranks sixth on a list of the earth's most abundant substances, comprising just under three percent of the earth's crust. In its pure (elemental) form, sodium is a silvery-white color and is classified as a metal. Despite being a metal, sodium is in fact quite soft and can even be cut with a knife. However, it is unlikely that you will ever in your daily life encounter this elemental form of sodium, as it reacts fiercely with oxygen and even water. Because of sodium's high reactivity with these common substances, it is not found in nature in its elemental form (i.e. pure sodium). Instead, sodium is found in nature combined with one of several other substances.

The most familiar form of sodium we all come in contact with is table salt, which is a combination of pure sodium and pure chloride. When an element such as sodium is chemically combined with an element like chloride, the two elements form a compound – in this case sodium chloride, or table salt. By combining with a second element such as the aforementioned chloride, sodium becomes 'stable' and is able to exist naturally in our environment. We'll discuss this property of sodium as being 'stable' shortly, but for now it's mostly important to understand that sodium must interact with another substance such as chloride in order to remain stable. Interestingly, while pure sodium reacts violently with water or air, attaching a chloride atom to sodium gives us the very common compound of table salt which – as we all know – dissolves effortlessly with water.

Sodium – just what is it?

So far you've heard sodium being discussed as an element, a metal, and a compound. Yet you've also probably heard of sodium as being one part of your daily intake of vitamins and minerals. What exactly then is sodium – an element, metal, compound, or mineral? Factually speaking, sodium itself is both an element and a metal. In fact, within that nightmarish chart from back in high school – known better as the periodic table of elements – you'll see that sodium falls in at atomic number 11. Based on its position within the periodic table, sodium is classified as a "Group 1" element, which indicates that it belongs to the alkali metals (more on alkali shortly). If sodium is both an element and a metal, how do classifications as a compound and a mineral factor in? That label is a little more misleading yet is still quite relevant to this discussion.

As we discussed, pure sodium's highly reactive state does not allow it to exist naturally in its elemental form.

Therefore, the sodium atom joins with other atoms such as chloride in order to share electrons and exist as one of over 100 compounds (i.e. a substance of two separate elements) such as sodium bicarbonate or monosodium glutamate, many of which are utilized by the food industry [2]. This use of sodium in the health and food industry is where we often hear about the last classification of sodium – as a mineral. Minerals are compounds that occur naturally in nature. As such, sodium itself (in its pure form) is not actually a mineral; however, it is part of the compound *sodium chloride* that our bodies seem to be inundated with every day as a result of the foods that we eat. Therefore, sodium chloride – not sodium – is the actual mineral that is responsible for your daily sodium intake.

If this all seems a bit confusing, don't worry. It's not likely that you will be corrected for calling sodium a mineral, but it is important for understanding the small differences of each in outlining the true nature of sodium. Other sodium compounds (e.g. sodium bicarbonate) are also consumed that provide a source of sodium, but these other compounds are rarely consumed at a level comparable to our intake of sodium chloride. Regardless, referring to sodium itself as either a compound or a mineral is somewhat of a misnomer, as what you are actually consuming is one of the compound forms of the basic element of sodium.

Sodium Sources

Supplying our demand for salt requires us to harvest it from its source and put its raw form through a series of processes in order to produce the particular sodium compound desired. We have touched on a couple of the various sodium compounds that we come into contact with such as sodium chloride. Whereas there are so many natural sodium compounds it would take many, many chapters – if not books – to outline the source and processing procedures of all of them. Because sodium chloride is the most common of these compounds, in addition to its influence on our health and its vast use in the food industry, we will focus mainly on this specific compound for outlining the source of sodium.

As discussed, we encounter sodium in many forms throughout the day. Most often we think of food-based relationships with sodium such as the sodium added to our food, but there are many other ways that we encounter sodium. For example, unless you have spent your life in the 'deep south' part of the country, you've likely seen large dump trucks carrying loads of road salt in the winter. Road salt is essentially unrefined sodium chloride known as halite, sometimes mixed with a few added chemicals to prevent the road salt from sticking together (i.e. "caking"). Road salt is spread on roads to help melt hazardous road ice and also to prevent ice from forming. The immense roadway system which supports our economy requires tens of millions of tons per year – quite a hefty amount by any standard [1].

Where does all of this sodium chloride come from? Perhaps more importantly, how do we obtain it? As mentioned, sodium chloride is all around us in the earth's crust, albeit in a highly unrefined form. The process for obtaining sodium chloride has not changed much since it was

41

initially used as a food additive thousands of years ago. It is thought that the Minoan civilization was the first to harness the sun to evaporate sea water in order to harvest the remaining salt over 3,000 years ago [3]. In fact, harvesting of salt from seawater sources was a lucrative enough business to pay for Columbus' journey across the ocean [3]! Therefore, it could be said that America was discovered largely on the lucrative business of salt harvesting.

Seawater evaporation was historically the most common method for harvesting salt, but it is not as popular now due to present-day mining techniques such as solution mining or harvesting directly from rock salt deposits. Solution mining involves flushing underground sodium chloride deposits with water that dissolves the salt and other materials into a briny solution. This solution is then pumped up to the surface to allow for evaporation. Similarly, rock salt deposits deep underground are mined, where the rock salt itself is brought to the surface and processed. The sheer size of these underground deposits combined with the limitless concentration of salt in our oceans provides what is essentially an endless supply of salt for everything from road de-icing to human consumption.

Of the mined sodium chloride, approximately 36% is used in the chemical industry for various processes such as what is needed for the extraction of chloride [6]. When pure sodium is needed for various chemical processes (e.g. laboratory experiments), it is typically obtained through the electrolysis of mined sodium chloride. Another 44% is relegated to road de-icing. The remaining 20% is designated for use in the food and agriculture industry. Interestingly, less than one percent of mined salt ends up as actual table salt.

No matter the source of the sodium that reaches our food industry, our health is dependent in large part upon consuming an adequate amount of sodium to allow our bodies to carry out the complex physiological processes required for daily life. However, these processes occur not as a result of the sodium chloride compound alone, but instead from the power held within the unimaginably small sodium atom. To grasp the amazing properties of the sodium atom and understand how our bodies capture and utilize these properties we must examine briefly the sodium atom itself in order to understand its immense capabilities.

Structure of Sodium

So far we've talked about what sodium is and how it is typically found in nature. In order to appreciate how sodium exerts its effects on our bodies – and in turn our health – we need to take a look at the structure of sodium. For that, we must divert our attention into the ominous world of atomic structure. Let's pause a moment and let that cold chill work its way down your spine before we continue, shall we? Actually, don't bother. We're not heading off into a graduate-level biophysics lecture here. Rather, we're going to take a moment to get a quick overview of the important properties of the sodium atom that ultimately allow it to interact with other elements as well as our body. Remember, without an understanding of the basics of sodium we can't fully understand how a low-sodium lifestyle can improve our health. So, take a deep breath, grit your teeth, and hold on as we take a look at just what it is that makes the sodium atom so fascinating.

As an individual element we will typically hear sodium described as an atom. While this is true, the functionality of sodium occurs when sodium is in its ion (or ionic) form. An ion is an atom that shares one or more of its electrons with another element to form a compound. For example, when a

Sodium as an atom

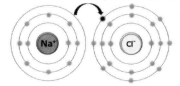

Sodium as an ion (with chloride)

Figure 2.1. Sodium (Na) shown as an element (top), and in its ionic form (bottom) as it shares its outer electron with chloride (Cl) to form the compound sodium chloride, or "table salt".

sodium atom binds with a chloride atom, the sodium atom becomes an ion as it shares an electron with chloride to form sodium chloride (Figure 2.1). In sharing one of its negatively-charged electrons, the sodium ion creates an imbalance between its protons and electrons because no longer are the atom's positively-charged protons cancelled out by the negatively-charged electrons. Instead – using the sodium chloride example – sodium's donation of one electron to chloride leaves it with more protons than electrons, in turn giving the sodium ion an overall positive charge. As we will see in the next chapter, the sodium ion's resulting positive charge is what is harnessed by our bodies to perform several vital functions. Without this positive charge, living organisms would not have the ability to generate nerve impulses or muscle contractions, along with several other vital tasks which we will discuss further in the next chapter.

The basics of pH

Now that we have looked at the structure of sodium we can begin to look at how this structure allows sodium to influence its environment. It is important to note that although this topic would seem best suited for a chemistry textbook, the influence that sodium has on your health is directly tied into these structural properties. Furthermore, because going low-sodium is largely dependent upon your food choices, it is imperative to outline how these sodium-related processes influence food preparation, cooking, and basic physiology of the body. Therefore, we will next look at some basic concepts that both outline ion concentrations and influence the movement of sodium within the body.

As mentioned earlier, sodium's role in the food industry includes helping to improve food taste as well as extend shelf-life. In both of these cases, sodium is added in order to improve on some feature of the food (i.e. taste), but sodium is not actually *required* for that food to exist. This is important to understand, as many foods that we eat do in fact require sodium in order to exist. We have all likely had a food at some point in our lives that didn't taste quite right until we added a little salt. Prior to my low-sodium lifestyle that included for me pretty much any cooked vegetables, meat, and even foods such as soups that already had a high amount of sodium included. In hind sight, I now wonder if I really needed to add the salt or if it was moreover some sort of ingrained habit that resulted in my desire to add salt. Regardless of the reason, I – like so many others – added salt to foods or recipes for flavor enhancement only, instead of adding the salt as some required component of a recipe.

The use of salt for seasoning is not its only need in a recipe, though, as certain sodium-based compounds are necessary to generate a reaction that is an essential part of the food's production. For example, quick breads (e.g. banana bread) require compounds like baking soda in the ingredient list because of the compound's ability to generate a specific reaction. To understand how all of this works we need to consider a phenomenon commonly known as 'potential hydrogen', or "pH". In relatively scary science terms, pH represents the negative log of hydrogen concentration in a water solution. In less scary terms, pH is the concentration of hydrogen ions present in a solution. As hydrogen ion concentration increases, the pH becomes more acidic. Conversely, as hydrogen ion concentration decreases, the solution becomes less acidic.

Luckily for us, pH is relatively easy to understand when you view it as a scale. Measuring pH occurs on a scale of 0 – 14, with a value of seven being considered a "neutral pH" such as what exists in pure water (Figure 2.2). When pH values are less than "7", that solution or substance is considered acidic and classified as an acid. As just mentioned, acidity represents an increasing concentration of hydrogen ions (H+) in a solution, such that the stronger the acid – or 'lower' the pH value – the greater the concentration of hydrogen ions in the

Figure 2.2. The pH scale indicates degree of acidity (moving towards "0") or alkalinity (moving towards "14"), with solutions having a pH of "7" being considered neither acidic nor basic.

solution. As you move from right to left in the acidic range (or from seven to zero on the scale), each value becomes ten-fold more acidic than the previous value. Therefore, a substance with a pH of "3" is ten times more acidic than a substance with a pH of "4". Examples of acidic foods range from highly acidic foods such as lemon juice or soft drinks (pH = 2.0 – 3.0) to much less acidic foods such as coffee (pH = 5.0 – 6.0) or milk (pH 6.5-6.7).

When pH values exceed 7.0, their classification changes from that of an acid to that of a base, or 'alkaline' substance. The higher the base or "alkalinity", the greater the concentration of hydroxide ions (OH-) in the solution (Figure 2.3). Therefore, values in the alkaline range increase in alkalinity as the pH value increases above "7". Similar to acidity (but in reverse order) an alkaline food with a pH of "8" is ten times more alkaline than one of pH "7". Some examples of alkaline foods include watermelon and broccoli (pH = 9.5) and wild rice (pH = 8.0).

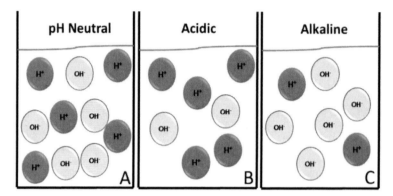

Figure 2.3. The solution in "A" is 'neutral' because there are equal amounts of hydrogen (H) and hydroxide (OH) ions. As the ratio of hydrogen increases in "B", the solution turns acidic, while a decreased ratio of hydrogen in "C" becomes alkaline.

Sodium Compounds and pH

Hopefully at this point you haven't started wondering if you bought a chemistry book by mistake. Though we are still in the basics of sodium, the application of pH will be especially relevant in Chapter 5 when we discuss how sodium-based products are utilized by the food industry, particularly how the addition of sodium compounds affects the pH of a specific food item. In order to understand these concepts, there remains a few more details that we need to cover specific to pH that will later reveal why sodium is so important in the food industry. Appreciating how pH influences food preparation explains why certain foods must contain sodium-based ingredients such as sodium bicarbonate (i.e. baking soda). The rationale behind such additives begins first in understanding what happens when acids are mixed with alkaline ingredients.

When kept isolated from each other, acids and alkaline substances are generally stable and can be quite boring given that they have no real activity. However, when acids come into contact with their alkaline counterpart – such as might occur in a recipe – a reaction occurs. You might have observed such a reaction first-hand in grade school when someone brought in their 'erupting volcano' experiment. If you were like me, all of the relatively poor design flaws were forgotten once your classmate poured vinegar down the volcano shaft, starting a reaction that likely left every one of your classmates in awe. What you may not have known at the time was that sitting in the bottom of the volcano was almost certainly an alkaline mound of sodium bicarbonate. When the vinegar (with its very acidic 2.4 pH) and a little red food coloring were poured in, a reaction occurred that we youngsters saw as some kind of amazing magical event that resulted in a spectacular outflow of "lava" in a spectacular eruption. Now, being a little more versed in the underlying reaction, we may be somewhat disappointed to know that the volcanic eruption was really nothing other than an acid reacting with an alkaline substance.

The degree of reaction between an acid and alkaline material is dependent upon the pH value of each. If a solution consisting of an acid is mixed with a similarly concentrated base, the two solutions neutralize each other as the hydrogen and hydroxide ions cancel one another out. However, if more alkaline solution is added than acid, the solution will turn increasingly alkaline. An easy way to think of this is to imagine mixing colors. We have probably all heard that yellow + blue = green. If pure yellow represents an acid, and pure blue represents an equally concentrated alkaline solution, the product of the two would be pure green. However, if instead of say a 1:1 mix of the two colors, a 2:1 mix of yellow/blue was used, the resulting color would be a brighter green due to the increased presence of yellow. In thinking back to pH rather than color, a 2:1 mix of acidic and alkaline substances would result in a rather acidic concentration with a pH well below 7.0 due to the higher concentration of acid.

Understanding these basic concepts of pH will serve you well when we later discuss sodium's role in the food industry. The addition of certain sodium compounds take advantage of the properties inherent to pH in order to generate reactions necessary for many recipes, especially in the baking industry. We'll save those details for Chapter 5.

Movement of ions

If you've made it this far after having survived discussions about atomic structure and pH, congratulate yourself for being persistent even through the difficult times! Having now outlined sodium's basic structure as well as the concepts involved in acid/alkaline reactions, we have just one more technical area to cover – the movement of sodium ions (i.e. ion transport) – in order to better understand how the body handles sodium once it has been consumed. Sodium, like all other nutrients, must be maintained within a very precise range in order to be used by the body for specific functions. Chapter 3 will outline how sodium influences certain processes within the body such as nerve impulse transmission, muscle contraction, etc. The ability for us as living organisms to perform these events requires careful regulation of sodium ions, particularly the ability to move sodium from one area to another, such as from the cell interior to the cell exterior, or from the bloodstream to the tissues. Therefore, we will close this second chapter with a look at three of these processes: active transport, passive transport, and osmosis.

When ions exist in an environment such as water, the number of ions in a specific amount of that water (e.g. 1 cup) establish a unique ion concentration. If you add more water without adding additional ions, the ion concentration in that new amount of water decreases. Similarly, if you remove water but leave the sodium ions, the ionic concentration increases. In the body, sodium ions are 'added' to the fluid in our body when we consume sodium, thereby increasing the sodium concentration in our body. Conversely, removing sodium ions – such as occurs through the process of sweating or urination – decreases the body's sodium ion concentration. Have you ever heard of someone cramping up after a workout and then being told that it's likely that their electrolytes are off? If so, you are intimately involved with the process of sodium ion transport. Profuse sweating removes sodium ions from the body, and when water – particularly water without added sodium ions – is consumed afterwards, the sudden increase in body fluid without a proportional increase in sodium ions causes existing fluid and ions in the body to redistribute using various ion transport processes. This condition of decreased sodium in the body, known as hyponatremia, ultimately throws the body's systems off, resulting in symptoms ranging from muscle cramps to even coma or death – all from drinking too much water and not consuming enough sodium after a sweaty workout! Now don't panic – hyponatremia doesn't occur in response to most workouts. You have to *really* sweat and also drink a *lot* of water after your workout, most likely more than you would feel comfortable with. We will outline hyponatremia more in Chapter 4, but the premise for how it occurs centers around sodium ion transport. Therefore, it is important to outline the process of ion transport in order to understand how ion levels are both maintained and manipulated in our body.

When two different ion concentrations occur in close proximity to each other, a *concentration gradient* exists. In our body, the cell membrane serves to maintain separation of two vastly different sodium concentration gradients – the interior and exterior cell environment. These environments can be represented by a water balloon in a tub of water. Think of the balloon as a cell with a very thin cell membrane. Intracellular fluid (ICF), which is present inside of your individual cells would be akin to the water inside of the balloon. Extracellular fluid (ECF) is the fluid that surrounds or "bathes" individual cells, just like how water in the tub surrounds the water balloon. As we have outlined previously, the concentrations of several ions including sodium can differ greatly between the ECF and ICF. In order for the body to function properly, these ion concentrations must be tightly regulated within both the ICF and the ECF.

Sodium concentration within the cell interior remains quite low while outside of the cell the sodium concentration is nearly 15 times higher [5]. Maintaining these separate environments is essential for normal cell function, yet our body's ability to precisely manipulate these concentrations is what actually allows us to exist – to breathe, to move, and to think. For example, activation of a nerve by our brain triggers an influx of sodium to the cell interior that must immediately be shuttled back out. Just that brief change in sodium ion concentration is all that is needed to carry a nerve impulse down a nerve! Or, when a cell membrane is damaged and the high exterior sodium concentration is allowed to remain for a prolonged time within the cell interior, cell death can result. The *controlled* movement of sodium ions back and forth between the internal and external cell environments must occur within very precise ranges in order to give us many of the physiological processes that we know. And, it is actually the *direction* of sodium ion movement that determines which transport mechanism is utilized.

When ions move from an area of high concentration to an area of low concentration (or 'down their concentration gradient'), the process utilized to move the ions is *diffusion*. No energy is required for movement of ions in this direction, a process termed "passive transport". Think of diffusion being represented as two connected rooms at a party. If one room is closed off, people will only congregate within the one room. As more people arrive at the party, that room becomes more and more 'packed', or concentrated. At some point attendees may begin to feel a bit uncomfortable as there is less and less room to move around. Eventually, the host opens a door to the adjoining room. What do you expect to happen? Most likely the partiers will start to move into the second room.   If following the model of diffusion, people will flow into the second room until the point where there are an equal number of people in each room, a point at which everyone is comfortable and has plenty of room to move around. Though this is a somewhat simplified explanation, it does detail somewhat the process of passive transport as it relates to diffusion and areas of high concentration.

As we will discuss in the next chapter, sodium ions will rapidly flow from the highly-concentrated exterior cellular environment into the low-concentrated internal cell environment in order to transmit a signal called an action potential, more commonly known as a nerve impulse. Because the cell membrane maintains separation of the low-concentration internal cell area from the higher sodium concentration outside of the cell, signaling the cell to open specific gates, or "channels", along the cell membrane allows sodium ions to rush into the cell through the process of diffusion. The opening of these channels has the same effect as opening that door in the party example above. When the door opens, people crammed inside the room will rapidly flow out of the crowded room much like opening a membrane channel allows ions to flow into the lower-concentrated area.

Unlike diffusion, where passive transport is utilized to move sodium ions from a high concentration in absence of any energy expenditure, moving ions from an area of low concentration to an area with higher concentration requires actively pumping or 'pushing' the ions into the higher-concentrated space. This process is termed "active transport".

Our cells perform active transport by using proteins embedded within the cell membrane to pump the recently-allowed sodium ions from the cell interior back out into the higher-concentrated extracellular environment where they came from. Unlike passive transport, active transport requires energy to push the sodium ions into the higher-concentrated exterior cell environment. Consequently, active transport requires an energy source such as adenosine triphosphate (ATP) to accomplish its mission. Thinking back to the party room, imagine that for some reason the second room had to be closed off suddenly. In such a case, party-goers may not be happy about going back into a crowded room. Therefore, security has to come in and physically coerce attendees to head back into the original room. Those security guards are effectively similar to the pumps that move sodium from an area of low concentration back to an area of high concentration. Just like membrane pumps require energy to work, the guards are basically 'extra muscle' to ensure that everyone gets out of the closed-off second room. Though no one wants to go back to the crowded room. Even though it requires a little extra effort, everyone eventually ends up back in the original room.

Let's use another example for this somewhat confusing process of active and passive transport and how they work in unison to maintain internal and external cellular concentrations. Imagine if you will a pond that you plan to drain. Being a caring individual, you want to remove all the fish out of the pond before you drain it. Therefore you plan to use a large net to gather the fish and move them over to a neighboring pond. As you move the net across the pond, the concentration of fish within the net becomes higher and higher, while the concentration of fish in the pond becomes lower and lower. The net, in this case, represents the cell membrane and maintains the separation of these two environments. Suddenly, a stump on the bottom of the pond catches the net and tears a small slit in the net. Fish start to find their way out of the net, leaving you the only option of jumping in to grab the fish and throw them back into the net.

Like fish would do in the torn net, sodium (and all other ions) will naturally move from an area of high concentration to an area of low concentration via diffusion until the channel (or hole in the net) is closed. Whereas the fish will try to escape the highly-concentrated net into the lower-concentrated pond, the process of diffusion allows extracellular sodium ions to naturally flow toward the lower-concentrated cell interior when the opportunity arises (such as through a leak or open channel in the cell membrane). However, getting fish back into the net requires a relatively high amount of effort on your part as the fish will not return to the highly concentrated net on their own. Similarly, sodium pumps must work (i.e. expend energy) to get the excess sodium ions out of the lower-concentrated cell interior and back to the highly concentrated extracellular space. Much like how you would need to spend energy to get the fish back into the net, the membrane pumps also need to expend energy in order to maintain or re-establish a concentration gradient. We'll discuss in the next chapter how this maintenance of the concentration gradient between the internal and external cell environments allow for many of the body functions that are essential for normal function.

The final type of ion movement we need to introduce is the process of osmosis. Remember the scenarios of drinking seawater and hyponatremia that we discussed earlier? These events capture the process of *osmosis* perfectly. Osmosis is loosely defined as the tendency for an ion to move from an area of high concentration to an area of low concentration after passing through a semi-permeable barrier. Although water can easily cross a cell membrane, ions such as sodium that are dissolved in the water cannot freely cross the cell membrane. Because it allows water to freely cross but does not allow ions to do the same, the cell membrane is considered a sort of semi-permeable barrier.

When sodium ions are present in a solution such as salt water, there are less water molecules in that solution than a solution with no sodium ions present (such as deionized water). The reason for this is that the dissolved ions such as sodium take up some space, and given that there is only a finite amount of space available, the same amount of water molecules cannot exist in an area with a high ion concentration in the same way that it could in an area of low ionic concentration. But, if you have a varying amount of space, such as might exist in the area outside of your cells (remember, the tissue can expand if needed), and you place a semi-permeable membrane (i.e. a cell membrane) between the two differing concentrations, water molecules will in fact cross that membrane in order to try to balance out the amount of water on each side of the membrane. Water molecules from the lower ion concentration will move toward the water with a higher ion concentration (and therefore fewer water molecules) in order to equalize the water molecule concentration on each side of the membrane. In our bodies, this process of osmosis occurs constantly in a variety of sodium-bound environments such as sweat glands and kidney nephrons (discussed in the next chapter). Remember that earlier example about seawater? When drinking seawater, the process of osmosis can ultimately become deadly. As it gets distributed within the body, the higher sodium concentration introduced into the body by the seawater will draw water out of individual cells in an attempt to balance the water concentration inside and outside the cells. This then begins, furthers, or accelerates the process of dehydration.

Conclusion

Sodium is a powerhouse of an atom. Through the seemingly small act of donating its single outer electron, not only are we able to exist and function, but we have a wealth of beneficial sodium compounds around us that we have been able to manipulate into various tools and processes that enhance our daily lives. For many of us in today's world our only conscious involvement with sodium comes at dinner time as we reach for the salt shaker. Little if any thought enters our mind about how our bodies utilize sodium or any of the other nutrients we consume. Regardless of whether we truly appreciate sodium's value, the impact sodium has on our daily lives is immense. And for some of us, failure to carefully monitor our sodium intake can have negative consequences. Despite these potentially negative effects, it is clear that sodium is essential in order for our bodies to operate normally. In the next chapter we will look in more detail at just how sodium is handled by several of our body's systems in order to regulate normal body function.

References

1. American Geosciences Institute (2017). Roadway deicing in the United States.

2. Heidolph, B., et al. (2011). "Looking for my lost shaker of salt... Replacer: Flavor, function, future." **56**(1): 5.

3. MacGregor, G. A. and H. E. De Wardener (1998). Salt, diet and health, Cambridge University Press.

4. Paris, J. A. (1831). The Life of Sir Humphrey Davy, Colburn.

5. Skou, J. C. (1998). "The identification of the sodium pump." Bioscience reports **18**(4): 155-169.

6. United States Geological Survey (2017). Salt: Statistics and Information.

Chapter 3 – Sodium's use in the body

In the previous chapter we outlined the basic properties of sodium as well as how the sodium atom interacts with other substances to generate its highly important ionic form. Now, we will look at how our body capitalizes on the properties of the sodium ion to perform functions that are essential for not only our health but also our daily life. For example, without sodium your eyes could not follow the text you are reading because the muscles responsible for eye movement could not contract. That's probably of little value however, once you realize that you could also not breathe, your heart could not beat, and your brain could not function without sodium. To outline sodium's involvement with some of these body functions, we will look at a few of the most prominent sodium-dependent processes that occur within the body and highlight how sodium's involvement makes these processes possible. By appreciating how our bodies utilize sodium we can begin to understand the need for this important ion and also recognize how our bodies handle the high amounts of sodium consumed in many of our diets.

Sodium requirements versus intake

It is important to reiterate that sodium is *required* for our bodies to function. Therefore, those of us adhering to a low-sodium lifestyle should not avoid sodium but rather work to limit our sodium intake. Given the amount of sodium most Americans eat, a reduction in sodium intake will still supply plenty of sodium to power those body functions that rely on sodium. As we'll see in this chapter, our body's need for sodium is constant, but the supply we provide through our diet is much more than needed.

When healthy, our bodies are quite adept at removing the excess sodium that many of us consume. The average American consumes approximately 3,400 milligrams (mg), or 3.4 grams of sodium per day [8]. Given this relatively high sodium intake, even cutting our intake by half will still provide ample sodium for what our bodies need to function normally. Still, many individuals maintain a high sodium intake each day, and upwards of six grams of sodium consumed per day is not unusual [7]. These high intake levels persist despite the Department of Health and Human Services recommending a daily intake of just 2,300 milligrams of sodium per day [3].

The 2,300mg recommendation is due in part to ensure that sodium intake replenishes daily sodium excretion from the body that occurs through perspiration, urination, etc. However, intake recommendations do not represent the amount of sodium *utilized* by our bodies on a daily basis. Rather, the recommendation is a mere suggestion for how much sodium an average healthy individual should consume per day. These recommended levels are most certainly much higher than the levels consumed by early humans, whose sodium intake came predominantly through eating meat and plants [6]. These early humans survived just fine on what is perceived to be quite a low sodium intake, so it seems clear that the body does not require a high sodium intake to function normally. How low is too low? That hasn't been determined yet and given the ethical dilemmas involved with determining how little sodium intake is necessary to trigger health problems, it may be a while before we know a true answer to that question.

Though we can't ethically establish a minimum amount of sodium needed by our body, we can look at what level our body maintains in order to achieve proper function. It is estimated that the sodium chloride content in a human body is 0.4% of the total weight of the body [5]. This would equate to a 150-pound person containing approximately 9.6 ounces, or 272 grams of pure sodium in their body – the equivalent of approximately eight tablespoons of pure sodium. Remember though, that this number represents the *total* amount of sodium in the body which in turn represents that sodium dissolved in the blood as well as that amount found inside of individual tissues within the body. Since we cannot precisely measure all of this sodium in order to get a person's actual sodium (or any other metabolite) value, and because the human body attempts to regulate sodium somewhat consistently between individuals, health professionals typically measure the content of sodium in either the blood or urine as a representation of what is contained within their body. For sodium, normal blood levels are considered to be between 135 and 145 milliequivalents per liter (mEq/L) while normal urine sodium levels fall between 40-220 mEq/L/24hrs [9]. When values fall outside of this range, several negative health conditions can occur. These conditions will be discussed at length in Chapter 4.

Sodium's role in the body

To help our bodies function, sodium performs two predominant functions in the body. Both rely heavily on the sodium ion's positive charge that we discussed in the previous chapter. As a result of this charge, sodium can exert a very strong influence on multiple body functions. The first function involves something called membrane polarity, a phenomenon that involves the balance of positive and negative charges on each side of a cell's membrane. Remember our discussion about how the internal and external cell environments have different charges and how those differences are maintained by the role of the cell membrane? In a moment we will discuss how sodium plays a predominant role in establishing these charges and also how precise manipulation of these charges is what allows us to move, think, etc.

A second major role of sodium in the body is to help regulate tissue fluid levels. This regulation of fluid includes blood as well as the fluid that exists within and outside of our individual cells. Both types of fluid are subject to fluctuation in response to changes in our body's sodium content, such as when we consume a large amount of salty food or when we experience heavy sweating or urination. Although blood and other body fluids are affected by our sodium levels, the underlying mechanisms controlling membrane polarity as well as regulation of body fluids first occur at the cellular level. Therefore, we will next look at sodium's involvement at the cellular level related to these processes.

Sodium and the membrane potential

As we discussed earlier, there is a significant difference between the concentration of sodium inside and outside of the cell, with sodium being approximately 15 times higher outside of the cell than inside [10], and this low concentration must be maintained in order for the cell to function normally. The existence of these two highly different extracellular and intracellular sodium concentrations in close proximity form the concentration gradient we talked about in the previous chapter, and are separated only by the cell membrane (remember the earlier example of the balloon in water). As we will see shortly, this cellular concentration gradient is critical to the normal function of the cell. In fact, if the gradient is not maintained – by keeping the fluid containing the high sodium concentration outside of the cell – the cell itself will die.

Maintaining a concentration gradient is the responsibility of the cell membrane. The makeup of this cell membrane allows water molecules to freely cross the membrane yet prevents sodium ions from crossing from the ECF to the ICF – or vice versa – on their own. In order for the cell to perform its required functions, however, the cell membrane must allow some external sodium into the cell interior by allowing sodium to cross them membrane. How? When a higher sodium ion concentration is needed in the ICF, sodium channels embedded within the cell membrane, are triggered to open. Remember the discussion from the last chapter about passive transport and that party room? Because of the high ECF sodium concentration that exists, opening of a sodium gate within the membrane causes a rush of sodium ions into the low-concentrated ICF via passive transport. This rush of positively-charged sodium ions into the negatively-charged cell interior creates a positive charge in the ICF, triggering a vital event called depolarization that we will discuss shortly.

The rush of sodium ions into the cell interior not only creates a positive charge within the cell but also means that sodium ion concentrations are now very high within the cell. As we noted earlier, sustained high sodium concentrations (along with other metabolites) within the cell interior can cause cell death. To prevent cell death from occurring, the cell must act to quickly remove the high sodium ion concentration from the cell interior immediately after a change in polarity occurs. By removing the sodium ions immediately after the ICF is changed to a positive charge, not only is cell death prevented, but the overall positive charge of the cell interior will be reverted back to negative. This removal of sodium from the ICF will serve to restore the cell's membrane potential back to resting levels.

Removing sodium from the cell interior, however, is not as simple as opening a membrane gate like when sodium ions are allowed into the cell interior. Because sodium must be pumped back to the highly concentrated ECF, energy is required to operate the pumps (think back to the example of trying to put fish back into the net). This is where adenosine triphosphate, or "ATP", is used to power the small proteins which pump out the sodium to the highly concentrated ECF using the active transport process. These specific proteins are embedded in the cell membrane and are commonly known as the "sodium-potassium pump" because each pump moves sodium ions along with potassium ions (which we will get to in a bit). Sodium-potassium pumps detect the suddenly-high sodium concentration within the ICF that occurs as a result of the sodium gates opening. These pumps begin to immediately move the sodium back out into the highly-concentrated ECF. By moving the sodium back into the ICF, most of the work required to re-establish the membrane potential is finished. However, we're not quite done yet, as potassium ions must be exchanged during this process as well.

We noted earlier that potassium is also present in high concentrations in the ICF when the cell is at rest. Much like sodium, potassium also has specific gates responsible for allowing potassium ions to move across the membrane. When activated, potassium gates (located in the membrane next to the sodium gates) open in order to allow potassium to passively flow from the highly-concentrated ICF out into the ECF where potassium levels are normally quite low. Now, about that sodium-*potassium* pump we discussed earlier – here you will see the reason for its dual-name. While pumping sodium from the cell interior, it also has a role in immediately pulling those just-released potassium ions back into the ICF, which is already highly-concentrated with potassium. Once completed and both sodium and potassium are back in their original highly-concentrated areas, the second half of the process to restore the cell membrane's potential is complete.

Though it can seem quite dizzying, the main point for you to understand about all of this membrane potential information is that the sodium-potassium pump plays a large role in maintaining sodium and potassium concentrations inside and outside of every cell. In other words, sodium is a vital component of the process that allows our cells to operate, which in turn allows our bodies to function. When working properly, the process of pumping sodium and potassium ions runs flawlessly at unbelievably high rates (approximately 1000 cycles per second *per pump and channel*). Though it seems to operate at an unbelievable speed, it may be more amazing to learn that this action goes on constantly, around-the-clock to keep us alive. Even more impressive may be the way in which the sodium-potassium pumps work as a unit to allow us to exist. But what you should also recognize is that this process results in the regulation of *charges*. Have you been told that your muscles and nerves work based on electricity? If so, what you should understand is that your cells' operation is not as much about electricity as it is about the precise regulation of positive and negative charges as we have outlined here.

I pointed out earlier that the temporary change in membrane polarity is described by the process of depolarization which lasts from the initial influx of sodium until that sodium has been removed back to the ECF. This process that we have just walked through is just one single cycle of a single channel and a single sodium-potassium pump that takes approximately 1/1000th of a second. Yet while this exchange of sodium and potassium occurs across a membrane, it only affects the polarity in the area immediately adjacent to each sodium channel and pump. In other words, the entire cell doesn't temporarily switch its charge from negative to positive, only that area immediately surrounding the channels and pumps. But this polarity change within the small portion of the membrane is highly important for sending signals both within a cell – such as down a nerve – and between cells, such as required for your heart to contract. So in reality, the action of a cell sending a signal is actually a series of these pumps working across the muscle or nerve tissue that allows our body to function. How then does this movement of sodium turn into nerve signal transmission or muscle contraction? The answer lies in how these pumps work in unison to generate a signal.

Sodium and the action potential

When any cell is at rest, the sodium and potassium concentrations are properly maintained in the ICF and ECF. For example, a muscle cell at rest cannot contract as the sodium and potassium concentrations do not allow the 'contract' signal to be sent from the brain. However, when you decide to activate a muscle such as one that controls your fingers, your brain makes the decision that sends the depolarizing signal down your arm. Remember our earlier discussion of this signal being 'electrical'? This is generally correct in that there is a small change in the positive and negative charge around a small portion of the membrane of your cells. What is actually transmitting the signal is the coordinated, precisely-controlled activation of millions of sodium channels and pumps that shuttle the positively-charged sodium ions around, along with other charged ions. When working in an orchestrated fashion, these channels and pumps create an action potential, one of the foundational mechanisms involved in cellular communication.

We have outlined that the exchange of sodium and potassium ions occurs around a single set of sodium and potassium channels and pumps. What becomes particularly interesting is that when one set of channels and pumps causes a depolarization of a specific area of the cell membrane (due to the flow of sodium ions into the ICF), that area of depolarization actually initiates depolarization in the immediately adjacent area of the membrane also! To imagine this – let's shift our focus for a moment and think of the contagious yawn. That's right, we're going to discuss the yawn here. Have you ever been in a lecture or perhaps been watching a boring movie and the person next to you yawns? If at that moment you had a sudden urge to yawn yourself, and the person on the other side of the yawner also yawns, you can somewhat see how an action potential can spread. As one set of pumps and channels changes the polarity in the immediate area of a membrane, it causes adjacent areas to depolarize as well.

To help further explain the process of depolarization, think of a line of three pairs of pumps and channels "A", "B", and "C" in a membrane. As the membrane around pair "A" depolarizes by allowing extracellular sodium into the ICF, the sodium channel in area "B" is triggered to also open up immediately afterwards. While doing so, area "A" begins to quickly start to repolarize its area by pumping the sodium back out of the ICF. And, as pump "B" starts its depolarization,

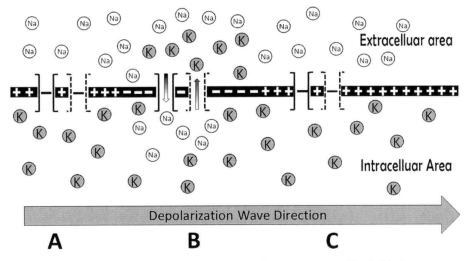

Figure 3.1. Sodium (Na) and Potassium (K) are normally held in separate concentrations such as over area "A" thanks to the cell membrane (thick black line). However, depolarization causes sodium channels and potassium channels (dashed lines) to open, allowing the ions to flow across the membrane to areas of lower concentratinos of each ion (Area "B"). This free flow of ions changes the polarity in the immediate area of those channels. The change in polarity causes sodium pumps (not shown) to start to quickly move these sodium and potassium ions back into their proper location relevant to the membrane, resulting in a return of resting membrane polarity.

pump "C" is triggered to begin, soon after which area "B" repolarizes (Figure 3.1). This wave of repolarization and depolarization continues spreading out in all directions across the entire membrane similar to how ripples on a pond spread out when a pebble is thrown in. This orchestrated process of polarization and depolarization through individual sodium-potassium pumps and channels is how our nerves send signals

71

and how our muscles contract. Clearly, this process cannot occur without sodium.

Sodium's role in fluid maintenance

Membrane depolarization is only one of sodium's two vital roles in our body. The second function draws upon the movement of ions in fluid that we covered earlier. Sodium's major role in fluid regulation within the body also results in sodium being named as the culprit for many medical conditions such as hypertension that are related to glitches in fluid regulation. Therefore, we will next detail the role sodium plays in fluid regulation by outlining how sodium is handled by our kidneys as well as our sweat glands.

We are all most likely aware that our kidneys serve to remove excess water from the body through the process of urination. While true, this does not tell the whole story of fluid regulation. At a macro level, your body's water level is a balance between fluids consumed (e.g. water, sports drinks, etc.), and fluids excreted, mostly through the processes of urination and/or sweating. Balancing this water content in the body is essential for normal functions like digestion, temperature regulation, and maintaining blood volume. Failing to replace body fluids lost through urination or sweating will require the body to shift fluids from one system to another in order to keep body fluids as balanced as possible. On an average day, up to a liter of water can be lost through normal processes such as breathing and sweating, in addition to that lost via urination. Even more fluid is lost when the body tries to maintain normal body temperature via the sweating process in response to strenuous activity such as exercise. Therefore, maintaining proper fluid levels within the body is an ongoing process requiring coordination of several body systems, of which sodium plays a key role.

Sodium content and fluid volume

For a cell to function normally, we outlined that the sodium concentration outside of the cell must remain constant in order for cells to function properly. Because sodium (and other ions) are dissolved in the ECF, the concentration of these dissolved ions must be controlled in order to maintain an osmotic pressure (remember back to osmosis and the seawater example from Chapter 2). Any increase or decrease in the sodium concentration of the ECF (which is directly linked to sodium intake or lack thereof) can in turn affect the osmotic pressure – and thereby the volume – of fluid in the ECF. This happens because osmosis will pull fluid from every cell's interior environment and move it into the ECF in order to maintain the proper osmotic pressure.

If fluid is removed from the cell interior to help restore the osmotic pressure, this creates a significant problem for the cell as it essentially dehydrates. This was illustrated by our earlier discussion about drinking seawater. In such a case where a high content of sodium is consumed, it will cause an increase in sodium concentration in the ECF. Based on the effects of osmosis, this higher sodium concentration in the ECF after drinking seawater means that there is a lower concentration of water molecules between the internal and external cell environments. To counter this, and to try to keep the water molecule concentration in balance, the body will pull water from the cell into the ECF in an attempt to return the osmotic pressure to resting levels. If this amount of water moved from the cell interior is great enough, it can dehydrate the cell to the point that it can cause cell death!

Because of this potentially disastrous outcome of moving too much water out of the cell, the body is tasked with regulating sodium concentration in the ECF so that osmolarity levels are maintained at a healthy level. This helps to explain your increase in thirst after eating salty foods. As your sodium levels rise in the ECF, your body can use the water you drink as a source for restoring the osmotic pressure rather than the more hazardous method of pulling water from the cell interior.

Sodium handling and excretion

Our bodies do not 'make' sodium. Therefore, increases in our sodium levels can only occur as the result of consuming sodium via foods or liquids. This is of course different than increasing the *concentration* of sodium, which can occur either via consuming sodium or decreasing our body's total water content without a similar decrease in sodium. Conversely, excretion of sodium occurs largely through urination and perspiration. To understand how sodium excretion works we'll next outline the structures involved in sodium excretion – the kidneys and the sweat gland – and how their structure and processes work to eliminate sodium from our body.

The processing of sodium via the kidneys is dependent upon your dietary sodium consumption as well as fluid consumption. Your kidneys filter approximately 45 gallons of blood per day and thereby process around 600g of sodium [4]. The vast majority of processed sodium is retained and sent back into the bloodstream while some is sent to the bladder for excretion via urination. Sweat glands, which excrete up to 500 milligrams of sodium per pint of sweat, can produce up to 12 liters of sweat per day [1], depending on factors such as an individual's core body temperature. Both systems are highly variable in the amount of work they do per day but must function properly in order to effectively remove sodium. To understand how the kidneys and sweat glands are responsible for sodium excretion, we will next outline the structure and function of these two systems.

Sodium and the kidney

Blood that has entered the kidney is filtered in a multi-stage process through one of a million or so nephrons in each kidney. Nephrons are the workhorse of the kidney and consist of the structures responsible for blood filtration, fluid reabsorption, and urine production (Figure 3.2). Blood that enters the nephron is first filtered by the glomerulus, a small 'bulb' of capillaries that contains an important structure called Bowman's capsule. This capsule has small slits that allow water and dissolved ions like sodium and potassium to pass through. This filtered material – officially called "filtrate" – then continues through the nephron as it passes into both the proximal convoluted (i.e. 'coiled') and straight tubule sections before moving on to the Loop of Henle.

The Loop of Henle contains a separate descending limb, thin ascending limb, and thick ascending limb sections. Here, sodium that was removed from the blood at Bowman's capsule

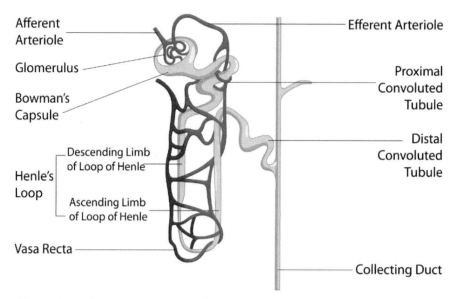

Figure 3.2. The various sections of the nephron are responsible for filtering the fluid of the body, including removal of sodium.

can be reabsorbed back into the body (if necessary) through sodium pumps located in the thick ascending limb. Any remaining filtrate then enters the final phase of the nephron – the convoluted tube – before being sent to the collecting duct as urine.

Because the thick ascending limb and distal convoluted tubule play major roles in sodium handling, this area of the nephron is typically targeted by diuretic drugs that are often prescribed in response to sodium-related medical conditions.

Certain diuretic drugs, for example, inhibit the activity of sodium-potassium pumps within the nephron. Inhibiting this pump results in an increased amount of sodium that remains in the filtrate for excretion, in turn reducing the total amount of sodium that remains within the body.

Hormonal regulation of sodium in the body

The removal of sodium ions from filtrate is largely regulated by a group of hormones that act on various areas of the nephron. When low levels of sodium are detected in the blood, the body releases renin – an enzyme secreted by the kidneys – into the bloodstream. Renin then initiates additional enzymatic reactions, ultimately resulting in the release of the hormone aldosterone from the kidney. Aldosterone triggers the nephron to increase the number of sodium-potassium pumps within the distal tubule and collecting duct of the nephron. As a result of the increased number of pumps, a greater amount of sodium is removed from the filtrate and returned to the blood which in turn maintains a higher sodium level in the blood than would occur if the additional renin-induced pumps were not active. And because blood sodium content can affect fluid levels within the body, this increased return of sodium to the blood also serves to help regulate fluid levels even if no external intake of fluid occurs.

Whereas renin is responsible for overseeing sodium regulation when blood sodium is low, there is also a mechanism to control for high blood sodium levels. When the body detects elevated sodium levels, such as after consuming a high-sodium meal, aldosterone secretion is inhibited. The resulting decrease in aldosterone reduces the number of sodium-potassium pumps in the nephron. Because of the decreased number of pumps, the high sodium concentration in the filtrate cannot be removed as efficiently by the existing sodium-potassium pumps. Consequently, the high-sodium filtrate continues on to the bladder where it is excreted in the urine.

A second hormonal response to a decreased blood sodium concentration occurs when increased osmolality of the blood (brought about by dehydration) is detected. When dehydration occurs, antidiuretic hormone (ADH), or "vasopressin", is secreted from the posterior pituitary gland. To counteract the resulting increased sodium concentration, the release of ADH into the bloodstream causes the nephron to insert water channels, or "aquaporins" into the collecting duct of the kidney. The subsequent increase in the number of aquaporins allows a greater amount of water to be removed from the filtrate and be returned to the bloodstream. This reabsorption of ion-free water helps re-establish the proper osmotic balance within the body, as the return of water to the bloodstream helps the previously-elevated blood sodium concentration to be diluted back to normal levels.

Sweat and sodium

The kidneys serve a major role in maintaining the body's sodium content by regulating the concentration of sodium in the filtrate which in turn helps regulate sodium within the bloodstream. As we outlined in the previous section, a high intake of sodium results in a decrease in the amount of sodium being removed from the filtrate. Conversely, low sodium levels in the body trigger the kidney to increase the removal of sodium from the filtrate. Though the kidneys serve a major role in removing sodium from the body, they are not the only system capable of directly influencing sodium levels. The kidneys are, however, the system that is activated depending on consumption of or lack of adequate sodium. Sweat glands, on the other hand, remove sodium independent of how much sodium has (or has not) been consumed. Each time our core temperature increases, the body triggers the process of perspiration in order to reduce our core temperature to normal levels. While perspiration is a very effective mechanism for cooling the body, it ultimately results in a loss of both body fluid and several electrolytes including sodium. In order to understand how perspiration can influence sodium levels we will take a closer look at the underlying mechanisms involved in the sweating process.

Whereas the nephron is the primary organelle of the kidney, the sweat gland is the main unit responsible for perspiration. Several million sweat glands can exist on the surface of our skin, and though each sweat gland is responsible for removing just a miniscule amount of heat, when summed together with all sweat produced from each of the body's sweat glands, the total amount of heat removed makes sweating a quite remarkable tool for cooling the body.

Sweat glands, specifically the *eccrine* sweat glands found on your skin, are composed of two primary sections - the

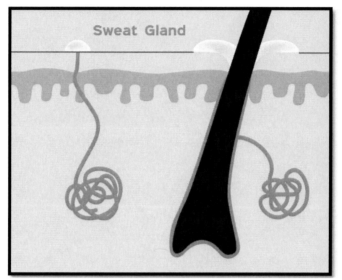

Figure 3.3. Sweat glands embedded within the skin serve to transfer excess heat from the body by removing fluid. Here, the highly twisted secretory coil of an eccrine sweat gland is shown on the left without its accompanying capillaries. A hair follicle is shown in black.

secretory coil and the resorptive duct (Figure 3.3). The secretory coil is buried deep in the skin and is surrounded by capillaries. The resorptive duct travels from the secretory coil up to the surface of the skin. In response to an increase in body heat, fluid is released from the capillaries into the secretory coil. The composition of this fluid within the secretory coil is predominantly water yet contains a high amount of sodium, chloride, and potassium ions. As the secreted sweat moves through the duct, the composition of the sweat is largely dependent upon body temperature. Initially, the sodium content of sweat within the secretory coil is essentially identical to the concentration within the blood (~3.3 grams of sodium per liter of sweat). However, as the sweat passes through the resorptive duct it decreases in sodium content. This decrease in sodium content is due to sodium-potassium pumps embedded within the duct removing much of the sodium as it passes through the duct. As a result of these pumps working to remove sodium, the resulting sodium content of the fluid within the resorptive duct is reduced by half or more (~1.6 grams per liter) when compared to the content of the secretory coil [2].

The number of sweat glands active at any time is largely dependent upon the body's core temperature. As core temperature increases, a greater percentage of sweat glands begin to release sweat. So even though much of the sodium originally released into the secretory coil is reabsorbed back to the body, any continued increases in core body temperature ultimately results in greater amounts of sodium being removed from the body. During strenuous exercise, when most of your sweat glands are active, 500 milligrams of sodium can be lost per pound of sweat. This is important to understand, for as we increase the number of sweat glands activated as well as the rate at which those glands are producing sweat, the amount of sodium excreted from our body increases proportionally. Your sweat rate, and the subsequent loss of sodium during sweaty activity, is unique to you; therefore, if you are concerned about sodium loss during exercise or other strenuous activity it is important to calculate your individual sweat rate. Doing so can help you replace sodium at the same rate it is removed through perspiration in order to keep your body functioning normally.

Conclusion

Clearly, sodium has a crucial role in the body. As we have discussed, the body's ability to regulate sodium is critical to normal function as it is vital for signal transmission and also for regulating fluid levels in the body. In healthy individuals, sodium intake is easily regulated through an equal excretion of sodium from the body. However, for some individuals the regulation of sodium is not adequately maintained. When sodium levels are disrupted in these individuals, a variety of negative consequences can trigger one or more of a variety of medical conditions. Therefore, the next chapter will focus on several of the most common medical conditions associated with sodium, including how sodium plays a role in the pathophysiology of each condition.

References

1. Bates, G. P. and V. S. Miller (2008). "Sweat rate and sodium loss during work in the heat." Journal of Occupational Medicine and Toxicology 3(1): 4.

2. Bovell, D. (2015). "The human eccrine sweat gland: structure, function and disorders." Journal of Local and Global Health Science: 5.

3. DeSalvo, K. B., et al. (2016). "Dietary guidelines for Americans." Jama 315(5): 457-458.

4. Féraille, E. and A. Doucet (2001). "Sodium-potassium-adenosinetriphosphatase-dependent sodium transport in the kidney: hormonal control." Physiological reviews 81(1): 345-418.

5. Harding, A. (2013). <u>Salt in prehistoric Europe</u>, Sidestone Press.

6. MacGregor, G. A. and H. E. De Wardener (1998). <u>Salt, diet and health</u>, Cambridge University Press.

7. Mahmood, A. S. K. S. A. (2015). "Assessment of Congestive Heart Failure Patients Knowledge and Compliance in Kirkuk." <u>Kufa Journal for Nursing Sciences</u> ‏‏مجلة الكوفة للعلوم التمريضية 4(2(‏.

8. McGuire, S. (2014). "Institute of Medicine. 2013. Sodium Intake in Populations: Assessment of Evidence. Washington, DC: The National Academies Press, 2013." <u>Advances in Nutrition: An International Review Journal</u> 5(1): 19-20.

9. Roy, K. S., et al. (2014). "Study on serum and urinary electrolyte changes in cerebrovascular accident." <u>Journal, Indian Academy of Clinical Medicine</u> **15**(2).

10. Skou, J. C. (1998). "The identification of the sodium pump." <u>Bioscience reports</u> **18**(4): 155-169.

Chapter 4 - Medical Conditions and Sodium

In developing this book, I had three types of people in mind that I felt would most benefit from its content: those that choose to start a low-sodium lifestyle, those that have a medical condition that requires them to be on a low-sodium lifestyle, and those close to someone who is required to be involved with a low-sodium lifestyle. While choosing to live a low-sodium lifestyle is certainly commendable, this chapter focuses on those individuals that fall into the last two categories as we will look at several medical conditions that are directly influenced by sodium. If you're like me and a medical condition drove you to start the low-sodium lifestyle, you may not have been told why sodium was the culprit but were instead simply told to cut down on your sodium intake. It's my intent that this chapter answers questions you may have as to how sodium affects your medical condition and why reducing your sodium intake can have beneficial effects. With an understanding of what is occurring within your body specific to the interaction between your medical condition and sodium, a clearer rationale can be revealed as to why it is important to adhere to a low-sodium lifestyle.

Hyponatremia

Fluid replenishment is a well-accepted preventative measure for everyone from athletes to those of us working outside in our yard. As we outlined in Chapter 3, our bodies require a specific fluid/electrolyte balance in order to function properly. Perspiration and urination naturally deplete fluid levels along with electrolytes, while consuming water and other liquids supplies our body with fluids that our kidneys must maintain within particular levels. For some individuals, however, medical conditions can affect the kidney's ability to remove water from the body. Consequently, the body's fluid levels increase. Hyponatremia occurs when the increased fluid levels rise to a point that dilutes the body's sodium concentration to hazardously low levels. As we discussed, reduced sodium concentrations in the body can be problematic for fluid regulation.

Though not necessarily a chronic medical condition that requires maintaining a low-sodium diet, hyponatremia can be a consequence of not consuming enough sodium. If you've ever had your blood sodium levels measured, you might remember that normal sodium levels in the blood are between 135-145 mEq/L. Hyponatremia is defined by medical professionals as a blood sodium level below 135 mEq/L [22], indicating that blood sodium has become overly diluted. Despite our body's ability to regulate sodium, hyponatremia is not exactly rare; in fact it is the most common electrolyte-related disorder encountered in clinical practice [21]. Under normal circumstances, the body would counteract a decreased concentration of sodium in the tissues by pulling from the 'pool' of sodium that can be found within the bloodstream. If an appropriate amount of sodium is consumed, that consumed sodium serves to maintain proper sodium levels in the blood and tissues, with any excess being removed via urination.

With some types of hyponatremia, the kidneys fail to remove excess water from the body. As we discussed in the last chapter, this retained water dilutes the body's sodium concentration significantly. If either the kidneys cannot remove the excess water (due to a disorder such as an inability to excrete adequate ADH) or the pool of 'available' sodium is inadequate to counter the increasing dilution of the tissue sodium, water begins to enter individual cells through osmosis. More specifically, the sodium content of the ECF may be decreased to the point that its level can become lower than the ICF.

Low sodium in the ECF changes the tissue osmolality, in turn causing water to move from the ECF to the ICF in order to balance out the water concentration. The movement of water into the cell causes the cell to swell up as a result. This process of cellular swelling is effectively the opposite of what happens when you drink seawater (with its high sodium content), as in that case the excess sodium in the ECF pulls water out of the ICF and causes the cell to dehydrate, or lose vital water. With hyponatremia, if the tissue swelling is severe enough or occurs in sensitive areas such as the brain, it can have fatal consequences.

Another type of hyponatremia is termed exercise-induced hyponatremia and can occur without an underlying medical condition such as diminished kidney function. This type of hyponatremia occurs when an individual sweats out a significant amount of fluid and sodium but fails to replace adequate sodium levels during those times when he or she is drinking fluid. For example, we all know that running a marathon would deplete sodium levels over time. However, the consumption of water at every aid station throughout the race can fail to adequately replenish sodium levels, in turn inviting the chance for exercise-induced hyponatremia to occur. Surprisingly, this "water intoxication" is actually a relatively common occurrence in athletic events. One study showed that in a group of Boston marathon runners, 13% of the 488 study participants were hyponatremic, and almost one percent of those had blood sodium levels less than 120 mEq/L [17]! Predisposing factors for experiencing exercise-induced hyponatremia in this group of runners included consuming a total of more than three liters of fluids during the race as well as consuming fluids at each mile of the race.

Findings from that study suggest that even during sustained, sweaty activity, hyponatremia can occur as a direct result of trying to prevent dehydration. Such information may make you think back to all of those advertisements and lectures you heard about staying hydrated during activity. Were they right? Absolutely! Exercise-induced hyponatremia doesn't happen simply by drinking a glass or two of water after mowing the yard or going for a jog. Rather, it is more likely to occur after drinking literally gallons of water after sweaty activity. If you're the type to drink a lot after activity, you can greatly reduce your chances for exercise-induced hyponatremia by ensuring that what you drink has a healthy level of sodium such as what you can find in sports drinks. Or eat something with a respectable amount of sodium (along with adequate fluid replenishment) in order to help maintain your sodium levels.

Because hyponatremia results from excess fluid intake (not excess sweating), treatment for hyponatremia typically involves withholding fluid from a hyponatremic patient along with administration of a diuretic drug until plasma sodium levels again fall within the normal range of 135-145 mEq/L. However, hyponatremia must be determined by a medical professional in order to ensure proper treatment.

Ménière's disease

Balance is a factor that many of us take for granted. When the balance sensors of the middle ear are off – such as may occur in response to something as minor as head congestion – your equilibrium can be affected to the point that you experience difficulty when standing in addition to a general feeling of dizziness. Ménière's disease affects over two million people [13] and is known to affect the structures of the middle ear that play a large role in balance. Though not as well understood as many other diseases, the National Institute of Health's National Institute on Deafness and Other Clinical

Disorders states that Ménière's disease is caused by a buildup of fluid within the bony labyrinth of the inner ear [16].

The ear's ability to detect head movement is a primary responsibility of the labyrinth system. Embedded within the bony labyrinth is a group of membranes that maintain fluid called endolymph. This endolymph is quite intricate and is designed to provide information to the brain about the both the head's position and any directional movements. In those individuals with Ménière's, excess endolymph within the labyrinth prevents the embedded sensors from properly detecting the body's movement and thereby inhibits the brain from properly sensing and interpreting the body's movement and instead triggers nausea, imbalance, and dizziness.

So how does a low-sodium diet influence Ménière's? The medical literature points out that the true underlying cause of Ménière's is still debated. However, it is thought that an inability to regulate fluid levels in the inner ear is a main culprit. The endolymph within the inner ear has an extremely low sodium concentration. Surrounding the endolymph is a fluid called perilymph with a sodium concentration over 100 times higher than the endolymph [9]. Maintaining this concentration gradient is relatively easy with a normal body sodium level. However, as body sodium increases such as after a high-sodium meal, the concentration gradient between the two fluid types becomes higher. Ménière's disorder is thought to result from either an inability of the inner ear to regulate these fluid concentrations, or a rupture in the membrane that separates these two fluids, which then allows the fluids to rapidly mix [10].

Ménière's symptoms are not consistent for all patients, but are typically grouped into acute and chronic events. Acute Ménière's events include "attacks", which are debilitating periods of dizziness, nausea, nystagmus (rapid eye movements), vomiting, and perfuse sweating that can last anywhere from less than an hour to more than a day. These attacks are typically followed by extreme fatigue along with "brain fog" that can exist for the next 24 hours or so, during which it can be difficult for Ménière's patients to concentrate. Chronic effects of Ménière's include ongoing dizziness and unsteadiness as well as increased susceptibility to motion sickness.

I am intimately familiar with the effects of Ménière's, as I outlined back in the opening of this book. Nearly three years of symptoms passed before I was finally diagnosed with Ménière's. My first set of physician's orders was to limit my sodium and also take a diuretic, both of which were typical recommendations given to Ménière's patients by clinicians [15]. Yet – to my surprise – sodium restriction is not consistent for improving the effects of Ménière's. Although many studies have shown that sodium restriction is effective for reducing the debilitating effects of Ménière's [18, 13], others have found that a low-sodium diet has no effect on Ménière's symptoms [1]. However, much like my initial (unsuccessful) attempt at reducing my sodium intake, I often wonder if Ménière's patients who do not have success with low-sodium diets are aware of the hidden sodium in so many foods that we eat.

Additional conservative treatment for Ménière's other than the typical recommendation of adhering to a low-sodium diet includes medications such as diuretics and the vasodilator Betahistine, avoidance of caffeine, and vestibular therapy. Other, more invasive treatment such as steroidal injection or surgical intervention are available options but will not be discussed here. For a more detailed look into Ménière's disease along with an overview of available treatments, I recommend that you read my book *Overcoming Ménière's*.

Hypertension

Hypertension is sustained, elevated blood pressure. Half of individuals over the age of 60 have hypertension in the United States [5]. Whereas blood pressure tends to increase as we age, it is expected that over 90% of adults will eventually become hypertensive [2]. When hypertension becomes chronic it ultimately triggers structural changes within the blood vessels as well as the heart itself [3].

Within the body, the cardiovascular system consists of the heart and associated blood vessels (arteries, capillaries, and veins). Adequate pressure must be maintained within this system in order for the heart to be able to deliver blood to the most distant tissues in the body. This need for pressure within the cardiovascular system is similar to what you may have observed when there was no water pressure at your home. When you turned on a faucet you suddenly found that instead of a rush of water there was nothing more than a trickle. Because of the reduced water pressure, which may have resulted from a broken water main, there was not adequate pressure to deliver a full stream of water to your home. In the human body, if adequate blood cannot be delivered to tissues such as your fingers or toes, you may have noticed that you lose sensation, or perhaps your fingers just feel cold. But if diminished pressure occurs in the brain you can experience lightheadedness when you stand or move, which can be problematic for causing instability or falls.

Obviously, low pressure is not the only problem that can occur within the cardiovascular system, as increasing the content of fluid within the vessels can trigger an elevation in pressure. As you probably know, the volume of the cardiovascular system does not generally change much under normal circumstances and holds around five liters of fluid (e.g. plasma, blood, etc.) at any given time. Increases or decreases in the blood's fluid levels – such as can occur through perspiration or drinking liquids – require the cardiovascular system to adapt in order to accommodate the change. If, for example there is excess fluid due to consuming a large soft drink, the body would normally excrete the excess fluid through the kidney. Similarly, perspiration results in removal of fluid from the blood. In both cases, the cardiovascular system must adapt to ensure that blood pressure does not increase or decrease above healthy levels.

Unfortunately, medical conditions can affect the body's ability to adapt to fluctuations in fluid levels within the cardiovascular system. For example, we'll discuss shortly how kidney disease can inhibit sodium removal from the blood. When that occurs, elevated sodium levels in the blood, such as can occur after consuming a high-sodium meal, draw fluids into the bloodstream. This in turn increases the amount of fluid retained within the cardiovascular system. As there is nowhere for the excess fluid to go, it triggers an increase in the pressure because the cardiovascular system is a closed unit – similar to a bicycle inner tube. If you increase the amount of air in the tube, the air doesn't simply 'spill out' the same way water might spill over the top of a glass. Rather, the pressure inside of the tube increases. This tends to make the tube more rigid and less elastic. Removing air from the tube – similar to how perspiration removes fluid from the blood – reduces the pressure and causes the tube to become more flexible. Remove too much air though, and the tube will become ineffective as it holds no useable amount of pressure.

Whereas an air pump is the regulator of pressure in the tire, the kidneys serve to regulate pressure within the cardiovascular system. Failure of the kidneys to remove adequate sodium or water from the blood can result in elevated blood pressure, in turn causing the associated effects of hypertension. Furthermore, hypertension can influence the depositing of fatty plaque within the walls of arteries that reduces blood flow through the artery [7]. This in turn serves to increase one's risk for a heart attack in addition to the presence of hypertension.

Depending on your own medical condition, you may have at some point been told that you need to lower your blood pressure. If so, you likely had a blood pressure reading well above the normal range. Hypertension is not an 'either/or' situation where you fully have it or you don't. Rather, hypertension consists of a range of values that determine your category of hypertension based on blood pressure readings as shown in the following table [2].

Category	Systolic (mm/Hg)		Diastolic (mm/Hg)
"Normal"	Less than 120	or	Less than 80
Prehypertension	120-139	or	80-89
Stage 1 Hypertension	140-159	or	90-99
Stage 2 Hypertension	160 or higher	or	100 or higher
Hypertensive Crisis	Higher than 180	or	110 or higher

The scientific evidence detailing a link between sodium intake and hypertension is hard to question. The success of the Dietary Approaches to Stop Hypertension (DASH) diet plan – which includes a reduction in sodium – has been instrumental in outlining a link between reduced sodium intake and a reduction in blood pressure. Even more importantly, this link revealed that the reduction in blood pressure was proportional to the degree of reduction in sodium intake [11]. Furthermore, another study indicated that a reduction in sodium can reduce the occurrence of hypertension by approximately 20% [20]. And, evidence indicates that elevated sodium intake correlated with an increased risk for cardiovascular disease as well as stroke [19]. These results provide strong evidence of sodium's role in hypertension, most likely due to its ability to influence fluid retention.

Kidney Disease

As we outlined in Chapter 3, the kidneys are largely responsible for regulating sodium levels within the blood.

When blood sodium increases, the kidneys respond by increasing the removal of sodium from the blood and sending it to the urine. Similarly, when blood sodium is low the kidneys return a greater amount of sodium back to the blood to ensure that proper sodium levels are maintained within the body. When functioning normally, the kidneys filter on average up to 150 quarts of blood per day and can produce up to two quarts of urine [12]. However, when the kidneys are not functioning properly due to problems within the nephron, their ability to regulate the body's sodium levels can be adversely affected.

Chronic kidney disease (CKD) affects up to 30 million people in the U.S., and many more millions are at risk of developing CKD [8]. Chronic kidney disease is classified as either kidney damage itself or three consistent months of a decreased glomerular filtration rate [4]. In CKD, sodium removal from the blood is impaired due to the diminished function of the kidneys. Because one or both kidneys can no longer remove sodium adequately, fluid levels tend to increase within the body, therefore contributing to the development of other conditions such as hypertension. Like hypertension, CKD has multiple stages of increasing severity, ranging from Stage 1 up to the most severe Stage 5 which represents kidney failure.

Stages 1-3 of CKD typically exist with minimal to no symptoms, which is likely why research has indicated that up to one in seven adults in the US has CKD [6]. Stages four and five are where symptoms usually appear with CKD, and as a result, patients in these stages typically require medical attention. In these later stages, symptoms often include muscle weakness and loss of muscle mass in addition to swelling in the feet and hands.

Because of the kidney's diminished ability to remove sodium from the blood, individuals diagnosed with CKD are often recommended to decrease their sodium intake. Current guidelines recommend a sodium intake of around 1,500mg for individuals with CKD [14].

Conclusion

Though sodium can play a role in a variety of medical conditions, in this chapter we covered the most prevalent of those conditions. What you might have noticed is that each of the medical conditions impacted by sodium are related to the regulation of fluid levels in the body. Because sodium has a direct impact on the body's fluid levels, *any* medical condition influencing fluid levels within the body is likely also impacted by sodium intake. However, patients can often capitalize on this relationship between fluid and sodium in that there is often a direct response in fluid level when sodium intake is decreased. This allows for a cheap and relatively simple treatment option for individuals affected by these conditions, as starting a low-sodium diet – as advised by a medical professional – can often result in a significant improvement in symptoms associated with these medical conditions.

References

1. Acharya, A., et al. (2017). "First Line Treatment of Meniere's Disease: A Randomized Controlled Trial." Journal of Lumbini Medical College **4**(2): 68-71.

2. American Heart Association (2016). "The Facts About High Blood Pressure."

3. Baumbach, G. L. and D. D. J. J. o. h. Heistad (1991). "Adaptive changes in cerebral blood vessels during chronic hypertension." **9**(11): 987-991.

4. Baumgarten, M. and T. Gehr (2011). "Chronic kidney disease: detection and evaluation." American family physician **84**(10): 1138.

5. Blaustein, M. P., et al. (2006). "How does salt retention raise blood pressure?" American Journal of Physiology-Regulatory, Integrative and Comparative Physiology **290**(3): R514-R523.

6. Chang, A. R., et al. (2016). "Using pharmacists to improve risk stratification and management of stage 3A chronic kidney disease: a feasibility study." BMC nephrology **17**(1): 168.

7. Dzau, V. J. J. J. o. c. p. (1990). "Atherosclerosis and hypertension: mechanisms and interrelationships." **15**: S59-64.

8. Fried, L. F. and P. M. Palevsky (2016). "Decreasing Prevalence of Chronic Kidney Disease in the United States: A Cause for OptimismDecreasing Prevalence of CKD in the United States." Annals of internal medicine **165**(7): 521-522.

9. Gagov, H., et al. (2018). "Endolymph composition: paradigm or inevitability?" **67**(2): 175-179.

10. Gibson, W. P. (2010). "Hypothetical mechanism for vertigo in Meniere's disease." Otolaryngologic Clinics of North America **43**(5): 1019-1027.

11. Jones, D. W. (2004). "Dietary sodium and blood pressure." Hypertension **43**(5): 932-935.

12. Jones, V. (2016). Incentivizing Live Kidney Donations: Economic Models for Policy Enhancements, University of Puget Sound.

13. Luxford, E., et al. (2013). "Dietary modification as adjunct treatment in Ménière's disease: patient willingness and ability to comply." Otology & Neurotology **34**(8): 1438-1443.

14. McMahon, E. J., et al. (2012). "Achieving salt restriction in chronic kidney disease." International journal of nephrology **2012**.

15. Minor, L. B., et al. (2004). "Meniere's disease." Current opinion in neurology **17**(1): 9-16.

16. National Institute of Health's National Institute on Deafness and Other Clinical Disorders (2010). "Ménière's Disease."

17. O'Connor, R. E. (2006). "Exercise-induced hyponatremia: causes, risks, prevention, and management." Cleveland Clinic journal of medicine **73**(3): S13.

18. Sheahan, S. L. and B. Fields (2008). "Sodium dietary restriction, knowledge, beliefs, and decision-making behavior of older females." Journal of the American Association of Nurse Practitioners **20**(4): 217-224.

19. Strazzullo, P., et al. (2009). "Salt intake, stroke, and cardiovascular disease: meta-analysis of prospective studies." Bmj **339**: b4567.

20. Trials of Hypertension Prevention Collaborative Research Group (1997). "Effects of weight loss and sodium reduction intervention on blood pressure and hypertension incidence in overweight people with high-normal blood pressure: The Trials Hypertension Prevention, phase II." Arch Intern Med **157**: 657-667.

21. Upadhyay, A., et al. (2006). "Incidence and prevalence of hyponatremia." The American journal of medicine **119**(7): S30-S35.

22. Waikar, S. S., et al. (2009). "Mortality after hospitalization with mild, moderate, and severe hyponatremia." The American journal of medicine **122**(9): 857-865.

Chapter 5 - Sodium's role in the food industry

Up to this point we have looked at sodium's properties, how it is used in our body, and some prominent medical conditions that are affected by sodium. These topics provide a foundation that helps orient us to the mechanisms by which sodium interacts with its environment, which can include the human body. Now, we will switch our focus to look at how we as consumers interact with sodium. In this chapter we will explore how the food industry exploits the basic properties of sodium by utilizing various sodium compounds (e.g. sodium chloride) to influence specific food properties such as shelf life or flavor. Given the vast role that sodium plays in food processing, it is important to understand the underlying rationale that makes the food industry so reliant on sodium.

It is the addition of sodium to packaged food items – not the natural sodium inherent to the food itself – that is the predominant culprit in our society's interaction with high-sodium foods. Few, if any, plant or animal food products could survive naturally if infused with the level of sodium that is added by the food industry. Regardless, the addition of sodium – either for flavor enhancement, preservation, or for influencing food texture – occurs in a majority of foods we eat. Given the prevalence of the food industry's use of sodium, a whole book could easily be written on this topic. However, we will limit our focus to discussing the various sodium compounds found in foods as well as sodium's influence in food preservation, flavoring, and the various ways sodium assists in the preparation of some foods. These topics will provide you a better understanding of why sodium is so prevalent in our food, along with a rationale as to why sodium is a required component of many recipes.

Sodium Compounds in Food Preparation

Remember from Chapter 2 that sodium as a pure element is highly unstable. Because of its unstable nature, sodium must combine with some other element to form a stable compound. In nature, many different sodium compounds exist that are used in various industries such as healthcare, cleaning, and obviously food. Given the vast array of sodium compounds used even in just the food industry, we cannot adequately outline all of them in this book. Rather, we will limit our discussion to those most common sodium compounds that we can expect to interact with in our food almost daily. It is important to recognize these various sodium compounds, as consumption of any of them ultimately contributes to our daily sodium intake. Therefore, we will next look at the most common sodium-based additives to understand their basic design as well as their influence on the preparation of food.

Sodium Chloride (Table Salt)

We have discussed sodium chloride at several points so far in this book, so we'll try to avoid any rehashing in too great of detail those aspects that we have already covered. Sodium chloride (or "table salt") is by far the most utilized and most familiar of all sodium compounds, accounting for up to 90% of the sodium we consume [4]. This is largely due to the fact that sodium chloride is comprised of 40% sodium (and 60% chloride). Despite real differences between salt and sodium it is not uncommon for the two words to be used interchangeably. Salt is simply one of many compounds of sodium, formed by combining a sodium molecule with a chloride molecule. It might seem somewhat ironic that a highly volatile metal (sodium) combines with a poisonous gas (chlorine) to form the sodium chloride compound that our bodies cannot survive without, but that is in fact what occurs at an elemental level.

Let's take a sidestep here and clarify the meaning of 'salt'. Obviously you know what someone else means when they say 'salt', but there are actually very different meanings for the word. To the consumer, everyone is familiar with those white crystals that we sprinkle on our food, and any mention of 'salt' in the kitchen will no doubt be referring to sodium chloride. But in a chemistry lab, mentioning 'salt' becomes a bit more complicated. In those scientific settings, a salt is any substance that combines an acid and a base that results in a compound with a neutral (neither positive nor negative) charge. For this book, though, we'll be referring only to sodium chloride in our discussions of salt.

It's important to point out the terminology as it also relates to use of the word *sodium*. Think about it – we are told to limit our salt, or that salt can be bad for us, or that we eat too much salt. In most cases, people are talking about *sodium chloride*. But, what people are referring to in terms of the problems associated with salt is likely that of sodium itself, which is just one component of sodium chloride. So even though the terms get thrown around a bit, it's important to understand which word you are referencing when discussing sodium and salt, even if the average consumer assumes that you are talking about sodium chloride!

Sodium chloride plays several roles in the food industry including not only food preservation and flavor enhancement, but also in helping food maintain its color as well as influencing food texture. Salt's diversity in the food industry is largely the reason that Americans consume almost twice the recommended intake of sodium each day, and nearly eight times the body's reported requirement of 500mg of sodium per day [1]. By far though, the two predominant uses of sodium chloride in the food industry are for food preservation and flavor enhancement (e.g. "palatability"). As we reviewed in Chapter 4, excess consumption of sodium chloride among those of us with certain medical conditions can have unfortunate complications, making it imperative that sodium intake is closely monitored.

Our excessive intake of sodium is not simply due to bad choices we make with the salt shaker. Over 70% of the sodium we consume comes from sodium added to foods during the manufacturing process while only 5% of our intake comes from salt added at the table [5]. Inherent sodium – that portion of sodium that occurs naturally in the food we eat – provides less than 20% of our sodium intake, still more than enough to supply our body's sodium requirement. In other words, eating whole, natural, unprepared and unpreserved foods such as fresh meats and vegetables would provide our bodies with ample sodium, with perhaps the exception of those who sweat excessively (such as athletes), as they give off excess amounts of sodium. Of all the sodium that we consume daily, sodium chloride supplied through various sources accounts for approximately 90% [4].

Sodium chloride as a preservative

For centuries, sodium chloride has been added foods in order to inhibit bacteria or mold growth, predominantly in foods with a significant moisture content. Naturally dry foods, such as beans, rice, or pasta generally have little to no sodium chloride added for preservation as these foods have a low moisture content. For most foods, however, their inherent water content provides an ideal scenario for microbes such as bacteria or mold to flourish. As food technology improved, the food industry became quite successful at utilizing sodium's basic properties to inhibit the growth of these microbes.

The method by which sodium chloride inhibits the growth of many pathogens reflects back to the simple process of osmosis that we covered in Chapter 2. By adding sodium chloride to the food (or the liquid in which the food is stored), an osmolality imbalance is generated between the high-sodium environment of the prepared food and the low-sodium internal environment of the microbe. True to the process of osmosis that regulates fluid in our bodies, the high-sodium environment pulls water out of the microbes, thereby killing the microbe. Similarly, when a high-sodium environment is not feasible for certain foods, even slightly raising the surrounding sodium content can be sufficient as microbes that are not killed directly must spend a great deal of their time and energy expelling sodium from their interiors. Just slightly raising the sodium content of the food's environment does not necessarily kill the microbes directly but inhibits their growth significantly, meaning that adding small amounts of sodium can be effective for slowing the growth of microbes in food.

It should be noted that adding sodium to prepared foods is not the only food preservation technique. In fact, improvements in food preservation such as refrigeration have greatly reduced the need for sodium-based preservation techniques, yet the practice continues. Unfortunately for consumers trying to lower their sodium intake, the use of sodium chloride as a preservative is simple and cheap compared to other preservation methods. Consequently, preserving foods using techniques other than the simple addition of sodium chloride will likely increase a food's production costs and may negatively affect the food's shelf life.

These days, it is common for multiple preservation techniques to be used by the food industry. Other methods such as altering pH levels, vacuum sealing (to remove oxygen), or using heat to kill microbes are often combined with the addition of sodium chloride to improve a food's preservation. For example, once subjected to minimal processing such as peeling or shredding, fresh vegetables may have a shelf life of only two to three days, even with refrigeration. However, storing those same vegetables in a sodium chloride or other sodium-based solution and also heating them during the canning process can keep the vegetables edible for two years or more, as is now commonly expected from any canned vegetable. By extending a food's shelf life through preservation, spoilage is reduced and food products from a single crop can be utilized for months if not years, thereby allowing for year-round consumption of foods previously available only in-season.

With a variety of other available preservation techniques, you might wonder why we should even continue to use sodium-based compounds to preserve food, or at least reduce our use of such high levels of sodium chloride in the brine if the food will also be cooked as part of the preservation process. While it might seem logical to simply reduce the sodium chloride content of a brine when preserving foods, doing so has shown evidence of increasing the risk of pathogens appearing in the food. For example, when the sodium content of chilled foods was reduced in the United Kingdom back in the early 2000s, a listeriosis outbreak was suspected to be linked to that reduction in sodium [7].

Listeriosis results from eating foods contaminated with the listeria bacteria, which can have severe health problems – especially for pregnant women. Separately, botulism risk is thought to increase when sodium levels are decreased [2], even when other preservation methods are utilized in conjunction with the addition of sodium chloride. This evidence presents a unique challenge to food manufacturers, as too little sodium chloride can reduce a preserved food's safety, yet too much sodium chloride contributes to those problems associated with high-sodium consumption.

Sodium chloride as a flavor enhancer

We have all heard at least one person say that foods are better with a little salt. Chefs often state that adding table salt reduces bitterness while also amplifying sweet and sour flavors. This type of thinking might indicate that all foods can benefit from the addition of sodium chloride, and at times it can seem that all prepared foods do include a significant amount of sodium chloride. It has been suggested that the historical use of sodium chloride in food preservation has played a role in our expectation for salty flavors, more so than a physiological need for sodium [2]. In other words, it appears that we don't *need* sodium chloride in the amounts that we consume in the same way our bodies *need* water when we're thirsty; rather, we seem to have just grown to appreciate and expect salty flavors in our food. A great representation of how much we have grown to expect sodium rather than need it can be found in the story of Vilhjalmur Stefansson, a professor-

108

turned-explorer who set out on an Arctic expedition many years ago. Initially, in eating unsalted meat with the Inuit, he reported the meats bland and lacking in taste. However, after continuing on an unsalted, meat-only diet for a few months, he noticed that his cravings for salt were gone, to the point that even when provided with a can of salt that initially contributed to what he wrote as the "best meal I had had all winter", by the next day he had forgotten to add any of the canned salt to his meal [8].

While we have stated that salt is really just sodium chloride, it's important to note that there are several types of sodium chloride out there. Specifically, if you've spent any of your time watching cooking shows you've probably noticed that the word 'salt' isn't used that often. More commonly you'll hear terms like *sea salt*, *kosher salt*, or *pickling salt*, among others that also include table salt. But if all of these salts are just sodium chloride, what is the real difference? The answer depends on how you want to analyze that question. From a true analysis, yes, there is a difference as sea salt is generally unrefined and therefore has several additional minerals (e.g. zinc, potassium, etc.) that are left over from evaporated sea water. You will also find differences in texture, grain size, and color between the various types of salt. From a low-sodium perspective, however, there is really no difference as every type of sodium-chloride used in the food industry (even the brightly-colored types that might seem too pretty to eat) adds effectively the same level of sodium to the diet and can therefore have a negative influence on certain sodium-related health conditions.

Generally, when people take on a low-sodium diet their desire for a salty taste tends to fade over time [2]. And as you might expect, individuals who are exposed to higher-salt diets tend to crave more sodium chloride in their food over time. Interestingly, reduced sodium consumption at a young age leads to reduced blood pressure as teenagers [2], suggesting that reduced exposure to sodium leads to a reduced desire for – or at least an intake of – sodium in later years. This collection of evidence further indicates that not only do we not seem to need the amount of sodium we typically consume, but reducing consumption of sodium at a young age tends to lead to reduced consumption at a later age. Both of these considerations are vital as they lend evidence as to why we as a society tend to have high sodium intakes.

Speaking of salty taste – have you ever wondered how our bodies are able to detect salt flavors? In other words, if I put a white, crystallized substance in the palm of your hand, why is it that your hand cannot tell you if it is salt or sugar, yet if I put just a few grains of each on your tongue, within seconds you can recognize it? The answer is that our skin does not contain the proper sodium detectors (i.e. receptors) that we find on our major taste-sensor: the tongue. Along the surface of our tongue are taste buds, and on each taste bud are specialized cells that are designed for each of the taste sensations (e.g. sweet, salty, etc.). Sodium chloride perception occurs when a sodium ion in the food that you eat comes into contact with a sodium channel – specifically, the epithelial sodium channel that is similar to the sodium channels we discussed in Chapter 3. As sodium passes through this channel, it activates a nerve pathway that tells the brain that the food is salty. It is important, however, to distinguish the perception of sodium – which occurs at the tongue – from the actual absorption of sodium that takes place within the digestive tract. Receptors on the tongue only tell the brain that the food is salty. For sodium to get into the body and trigger events such as fluid retention, the salty food must first be consumed and then be digested and absorbed within the intestines.

Understanding sodium chloride taste perception has a unique link to both the food industry and sodium intake. As one example, the size of sodium chloride crystals used on a food can influence sodium consumption. Like any soluble crystals such as those found in sugar or salt, the larger the crystal, the longer that crystal takes to fully dissolve. The dissolving of salt is important in the food industry, as for salty flavor to be detected the crystal must first be dissolved into a liquid. For a quick example, dry your tongue off with a towel and then put a few crystals of sodium chloride onto your dry tongue. Because there is no liquid (usually provided by the food or your saliva) that will help the sodium chloride dissolve into separate sodium and chloride ions, the crystals cannot release its sodium ions into the sodium channel. Put a few drops of water on those crystals, however, and almost instantly you will detect the salty flavor. This illustrates how moisture – contained either within the food or in your saliva – helps dissolve the sodium chloride in food and allows the sodium to be detected by your brain. Relating this back to the food industry, smaller sodium chloride crystals are more easily dissolved. Larger crystals – such as you might find on a classic pretzel – begin to release sodium ions once in your mouth but those same crystals may not be fully dissolved during the process of chewing. As a result, the remaining (undissolved) crystals are swallowed even though the salty flavor was detected, meaning that *unnecessary, excess sodium was consumed*. By using smaller salt crystals a salty flavor can be detected but with an overall lower sodium content of the food [2].

Sodium bicarbonate (baking soda)

Despite not being quite as widespread as sodium chloride, there's little doubt you're familiar with sodium bicarbonate and you have probably consumed it at some point in the previous 24 hours. The reason for your likely recent consumption of sodium bicarbonate is somewhat dependent upon whether you were hungry or ill, as sodium bicarbonate is used in the food industry as well as the medical field. Unlike sodium chloride, however, sodium bicarbonate is not typically added to food in order to improve taste; rather, it has a specific purpose that is focused largely on the science of pH that we outlined in Chapter 2. To outline this characteristic, we will next outline the vital role sodium bicarbonate plays in food preparation. This is important, for much like sodium chloride, consuming foods that utilize sodium bicarbonate will directly influence your daily sodium consumption. Understanding sodium bicarbonate's role in the food industry will in turn allow you to recognize those foods that likely include sodium bicarbonate in their ingredient list.

Sodium bicarbonate, or 'baking soda', is not found naturally but is rather the product of a series of refinements. The production of baking soda typically starts with the mining of the mineral trona [10]. Trona is then refined into soda ash, or "calcium carbonate" before being again refined into sodium bicarbonate, a material of which contains approximately 30% sodium. Sodium bicarbonate is an important additive for many foods such as bread, mostly for its leavening capability which we will discuss later. Sodium bicarbonate is also highly effective in reducing stomach acid associated with gastric reflux, ulcers, and indigestion; hence the possibility that you consumed sodium bicarbonate as part of your medical treatment. On a related note, your pancreas produces sodium bicarbonate in order to counteract the effects of acid in your body. This helps protect the small intestine from damage induced by stomach acid in addition to keeping your blood from getting too acidic during strenuous bursts of activity (think back to the pH discussion in Chapter 2).

As mentioned above, sodium bicarbonate is not a preservative or flavor enhancer but is added to foods for its influence on food texture. As we will discuss shortly, sodium bicarbonate's role in a recipe is largely what makes the difference in baked goods between a light, fluffy cake and a disastrous blob of solid dough. Personally, because of its importance in food texture I make a larger allowance in my own dietary intake for sodium bicarbonate than I do sodium chloride. In other words, I am more willing to consume a product that has sodium bicarbonate as its primary source of sodium than I am one that has sodium chloride as its source of sodium, mostly because I know that the sodium bicarbonate has a legitimate need to be in the food item as it often provides the structure required for a specific chemical reaction that gives many baked goods their 'airy' texture. Simply put, many recipes could not occur without sodium bicarbonate, while recipes that add sodium chloride for flavoring or preservation can still occur even without the sodium chloride.

If you remember back to our overview of pH, we discussed how mixing an acid and a base produce water as well as a salt such as sodium chloride. While that type of reaction may get chemists to perk up a bit, you might think that such an event would have little importance to the food industry. In actuality, you would be quite wrong. The beauty of this reaction for the food industry is that we have found a way to manipulate the components of an acid/base reaction so that we take advantage of a specific by-product, such as carbon dioxide, that is beneficial in food preparation – such as one that produces small pockets of gas in a batter. As the batter firms up, those small pockets get trapped, in turn creating millions of little air bubbles within the food item. This rationale is precisely why baking soda is a vital part of certain recipes such as cake mixes.

Baking soda has a pH of around 8.4 in water. When it reacts with an acid such as milk or lemon juice that is also an ingredient in a recipe, the molecular composition of the alkaline baking soda reacting with the other acidic ingredients generates carbon dioxide. Within cake batter or cookie dough, the ongoing generation of small carbon dioxide 'bubbles' during the baking process is what typically creates those tiny dough pockets we are familiar with.

It is important to understand that baking soda provides the same relative effect as yeast, given that both leavening agents work by releasing carbon dioxide. However, yeast is used when the dough is allowed to 'rise', and is not typically used in various baked goods such as cakes, desserts, or pancakes. In a strange twist of fate, it might be thought that yeast-leavened food products would be lower in sodium content as yeast-derived breads typically don't include baking soda in the recipe. Unfortunately, the lack of baking soda in many yeast-based foods are cancelled out by the inclusion of sodium chloride in bread recipes. This addition of sodium chloride to yeast-based dough is recommended not only to add flavor to the bread but also to help with strengthening the dough by influencing the gluten contained in the flour. Whether it's for leavening or flavor addition, baked goods rely heavily on sodium compounds for their texture.

Sodium bicarbonate + Acids (Baking powder)

Using the same premise as baking soda, baking powder is designed to react and produce carbon dioxide and is often used when there is no acid present in a recipe such as often occurs in cookies or cakes. As discussed, baking soda is comprised of just sodium bicarbonate, and as it consists of just a simple base it must react with something in a batter comprised of an acidic (i.e. below 7.0 pH) nature. Baking powder, on the other hand, contains baking soda along with a dry acidic component such as cream of tartar (pH of 5.0). In other words, baking powder contains both an acid and a base in an inactivated (i.e. dry) state. To help maintain its dry state while on the shelf, cornstarch is often included as an inert ingredient to help prevent trace amounts of moisture from initiating the acid/base reaction prior to use. During the cooking process, once exposed to a liquid such as occurs during the mixing of recipe ingredients, the baking soda and cream of tartar react to generate the carbon dioxide necessary for leavening. For an example of what happens when baking powder is exposed to moisture, put a small amount of baking soda in a spoon and then add a few drops of water – the reaction can be quite mesmerizing as you observe the direct chemical interaction of the two components.

Because the reaction of the base and alkaline solution occurs once exposed to moisture, it is important that the baking powder stay dry as long as possible. If exposed to moisture too early, the reaction will begin and may be exhausted (i.e. no more carbon dioxide produced) before the recipe's batter has set, such as might occur if you forget to preheat the oven. To get around the problem of generating carbon dioxide too early in a recipe, most baking powders in today's market are 'double-acting' and will include sodium aluminum sulfate (SAS) as an ingredient to help ensure that carbon dioxide generation continues throughout the cooking process.

Double-acting baking powders, which often substitute monocalcium phosphate for cream of tartar in order to reduce costs, cause a second reaction to generate carbon dioxide once

116

activated by the heat of the oven. Even though the acidic SAS is included in double-acting baking powder, sodium bicarbonate and monocalcium phosphate still begin to react immediately upon contacting a liquid (such as when mixing the ingredients). However, when the temperature of the batter reaches a certain point (140 degrees Fahrenheit), the acidic sodium aluminum sulfate reaches its melting point and then becomes available to react with the sodium bicarbonate at a temperature that occurs just prior to the dough 'setting' in the oven. This in turn means that the heat of your oven activates sodium aluminum sulfate, in turn triggering a second round of carbon dioxide generation when using "double acting" baking powders.

Although baking soda and baking powder play a vital role in the production of baked goods, their use is not without consequence to consumers who are trying to stick to a low-sodium diet. Baking soda, for example, contains nearly 1,300mg of sodium per teaspoon (about 1,000mg of sodium less than table salt). Baking soda dissolves into sodium and bicarbonate ions, so – much like sodium chloride – it plays a role in sodium intake and itself contributes to the 10% of sodium we consume that is not directly due to sodium chloride. Baking powder, on the other hand, is in effect a 'diluted' form of baking soda. As such, the sodium content of baking powder is much lower than baking soda, particularly double-acting baking powders that are more commonly available. One teaspoon of baking powder contains around 500mg of sodium, less than half of the sodium content of baking soda. Therefore, recipes which call for baking powder over baking soda will generally have a lower sodium content. Furthermore, recipes that call for both baking soda and baking powder can typically still be achieved by simply increasing the baking powder content to substitute for the baking soda. Luckily for those of us adhering to a low-sodium diet there are now sodium-free baking powders available that use the same premise as regular baking soda (i.e. carbon dioxide formation) but achieve it without the use of a sodium-based ingredient. We will cover sodium substitutes more in Chapter 6.

Monosodium glutamate

Monosodium glutamate (MSG) is a naturally occurring compound of sodium and glutamic acid (i.e. glutamate), one of the most abundant amino acids that we consume. Whereas sodium chloride is approximately 40% sodium, MSG contains only about 13% sodium, making it a much lower potential contributor of sodium to our bodies than the more common sodium chloride or even sodium bicarbonate. Unlike sodium chloride, MSG is not mined; rather, it is generated by simply combining sodium with glutamic acid. The FDA estimates that we consume up to 13 grams of glutamate a day [9] through our consumption of vegetables as well as protein-based foods including meats and milk. However, we consume only about 500 milligrams of MSG per day.

Glutamate exists in two forms, either 'bound' or 'free'. Bound glutamate is the naturally-occurring form that exists when a glutamate molecule is attached to a protein. Free glutamate occurs when proteins are processed during food manufacturing and in turn cause the glutamate molecule to be released. This free form of glutamate is the type that binds to receptors on the tongue. These receptors, when activated, provide the brain with a sensation of 'savoriness' (or *umami*), one of the five officially recognized tastes (along with bitter, salty, sweet, and sour). The food industry capitalizes on this property of glutamate and uses MSG as a flavor enhancer, as it is reported to improve the flavor of foods to which it is added.

Over the past decade, MSG has gotten quite a bit of negative press for a series of side effects ranging from headache to nausea. In fact, many grocery store items now include a "No added MSG" disclaimer on their labels. Yet, despite this generally negative attitude toward MSG, controlled studies have failed to consistently link these side effects to consumption of MSG [9].

Sodium benzoate

Sodium benzoate is formed by combining sodium hydroxide and benzoic acid. Sodium benzoate is found naturally at very low levels in several different foods including fruits, berries, coffee, and honey, as well as in cultured dairy products such as cheese and yogurt.

Sodium benzoate has been used as a preservative in the food industry for well over a century. Sodium benzoate has been shown to be most effective in acidic foods with a pH below 4.5 [3], and works by further lowering the pH of acidic foods to the point of making them uninhabitable to the pathogens that normally thrive in the food's naturally acidic environment. Soft drinks utilize sodium benzoate to increase acidity and thereby improve the taste of the high-fructose corn syrup.

Additional sodium compounds in foods

There are many, many more sodium-based compounds used in the food industry, and a comprehensive review of all of them would require several textbooks. Still, sodium compounds added by the food industry are the primary source of our sodium intake. The uses of these compounds in food preparation include emulsifiers, flavor enhancer, stabilizers, and thickening agents, among others. Most of these remaining compounds aren't a significant source of dietary sodium as you won't likely consume much, if any, of them on a daily basis. Therefore, rather than discussing each compound, we will list some of them out according to their general use in the food industry [6].

Emulsifying agents
Sodium pyrophosphate
Dioctyl sodium sulfosuccinate
Disodium hydrogen phosphate
Sodium alginate
Sodium caseinate
Sodium phosphate
Trisodium citrate
Trisodium phosphate
Sodium stearoyl lactylate

Anticaking agents

Sodium aluminosilicate

Sodium ferrocyanide

Neutralizing agents

Trisodium phosphate

Sodium sesquicarbonate

Sodium phosphate

Sodium DL-malate

Sodium dihydrogen phosphate

Sodium dihydrogen citrate

Sodium citrate

Sodium adipate

Aluminum sodium sulfate

Sodium potassium tartrate

Sodium acetate

Stabilizing agents

Disodium ethylenediaminetetraacentic acid (EDTA)

Disodium pyrophosphate

Potassium sodium L-tartrate

Sodium alginate

Sodium carboxymethylcellulose

Sodium caseinate

Trisodium citrate

Sodium stearoyl lactylate

Flavor-enhancing agents

Monosodium glutamate

Disodium 5′-guanylate

Disodium 5′-iosinate

Disodium 5′-ribonucleotides

Leavening agents

Disodium pyrophosphate

Sodium acid pyrophosphate

Sodium aluminum phosphate

Sodium hydrogen carbonate

Dough-conditioning agents

Sodium stearoyl lactylate

Sodium stearoyl fumarate

Thickening agents

Sodium alginate

Sodium carboxymethylcellulose

Moisture-retaining agents

Sodium hydrogen DL-malate

Sodium lactate

Sodium lauryl sulfate

Buffering agents

Disodium hydrogen phosphate

Sodium adipate

Sodium dihydrogen citrate

Sodium DL-malate

Sodium hydrogen carbonate

Sodium phosphate

Trisodium citrate

Trisodium phosphate

Texture-modifying agents

Sorbitol sodium

Sodium triphosphate

Pentasodium triphosphate

Disodium hydrogen phosphate

Bleaching agents

Sodium metabisulfite

Because of the many sodium compounds that are used in the food industry, many foods with relatively high sodium concentrations don't taste particularly salty as the sodium is tucked away in one of several sodium compound ingredients.

In addition to the sodium we consume through the food industry's use of these sodium-based additives, it's important to remember that another 10% of our sodium intake is supplied from food's natural sodium content. For example, milk as well as most meats contain a significant amount of natural sodium content compared to many fresh vegetables such as green beans. Yet even vegetables themselves have varying sodium levels. For example, carrots or beets contain a much higher sodium content than many other vegetables. These values should not alarm you though, as they are naturally-occurring sodium sources. Because your body requires sodium, the natural presence of sodium in most fresh vegetables, fruits, and meats should be of little concern. Rather, it's the food industry's added sodium that contributes to the vast majority of health concerns that we encounter. Furthermore, despite the already-high amount of sodium involved in food preparation as well as the natural sodium inherent to our foods, many of us add additional sodium through our use of sodium chloride as seasoning. When looking at this 'bigger picture' of food sodium content, it's quite easy to see why our sodium consumption is so high. It's also becomes clearer as to how much work can be involved specific to adhering to a low-sodium diet. In the next chapter, we'll take a look at a major ally in the low-sodium battle, the nutrition label, which is designed to help us identify the sodium content of a particular food item. In recognizing those foods high in sodium, we have the ability to make better sodium-based food choices that match well with our intended goals.

References

1. American Heart Association (2018). "How much sodium should I eat per day?".

2. Boon, C. S., et al. (2010). Strategies to reduce sodium intake in the United States, National Academies Press.

3. Cruess, W. and P. J. J. o. b. Richert (1929). "Effect of ion concentration on the toxicity of sodium benzoate to microorganisms." **17**(5): 363.

4.   Grimes, C. A., et al. (2016). "Dietary sodium intake and overweight and obesity in children and adults: a protocol for a systematic review and meta-analysis." **5**(1): 7.

5.   Harnack, L. J., et al. (2017). "Sources of Sodium in US Adults From 3 Geographic RegionsClinical Perspective." **135**(19): 1775-1783.

6.   Heidolph, B., et al. (2011). "Looking for my lost shaker of salt... Replacer: Flavor, function, future." **56**(1): 5.

7.   Roller, S. (2012). <u>Essential microbiology and hygiene for food professionals</u>, CRC Press.

8.   Stefansson, V. (1935). Adventures in diet. <u>Harper's Magazine</u>.

9.   United States Food and Drug Administration (2012). Questions and Answers on Monosodium Glutamate. United States Department of Health and Human Services.

10.   Wyoming Mining Association (2018). "Trona." 2019, from https://www.wyomingmining.org/minerals/trona/.

Chapter 6 - Sodium and the nutrition label

Knowing that sodium is added to so many food products, it requires a savvy mindset to ensure that the foods we buy adhere to our personal sodium guidelines. Years ago there was no indication of sodium content in prepared food; it was up to the consumer to try to figure out if the food might be high in sodium by looking at the ingredients. But as we all know, looking at the ingredient list on a packed food label can be mind-numbing. Though you might be purchasing something as simple as 'French bread', the ingredient list on the package probably reminds you more of some grade school spelling quiz than actual ingredients. While we might not be able to control – or even recognize – what ingredients go into the foods we buy, we now more than ever have the power to monitor the sodium content of these foods thanks to the detail outlined in the nutrition label.

In evaluating the sodium content listed on the nutrition label, we are afforded a relatively high level of control as to the amount of sodium that we consume. Personally, I look at sodium content before I even consider the price. If the food is cheap but contains a significant amount of sodium, that food has much less value to me as a low-sodium consumer than a more expensive but lower-sodium food that I can eat without concern of how its sodium might affect me. In this chapter we'll look at how to interpret and navigate the nutrition label to evaluate a food item's sodium content as well as how to use the information contained within the nutrition label to calculate total sodium in the food's container. We'll also look at the methods used to determine a food's sodium content, and why the method used is relevant to you as a consumer.

The Nutrition Label and food packaging claims

Through the 1950's and early 1960's, food was largely prepared in the home using basic ingredients. As food storage techniques improved, more processed foods began appearing in the grocery store. Unfortunately, claims made on the packaging ranged from confusing to misleading, and consumers had little confidence about what all was contained in the food packages. As such, the White House Conference on Food, Nutrition, and Health was organized in late 1969 to address the nutritional needs for Americans [1]. From this conference, the Food and Drug Administration became involved with food labeling of certain products starting in 1973. Back then, the FDA outlined regulations that required nutrition labeling only on two types of food products – those which specifically added nutrients, and those foods that made a specific nutrition-based claim (e.g. "low fat") on the label or in the advertising of the food [8]. So, if a food package made a claim such as "low in fat", a nutrition label would have to be included. Interestingly, sodium content was not required on the initial food labeling guidelines; instead, it was left up to the manufacturer as to whether sodium content would be listed on the label. Regardless, food nutrition labels weren't found on all foods at the time but rather only those products that fell under those two specific FDA requirements.

As health concerns associated with dietary changes began to emerge, the government worked to ramp up their research into links between food choices and health. Eventually, almost 20 years after the development of the first nutrition label, the Nutrition Labeling and Education Act of 1990 (NLEA) went into effect in 1994, requiring that effectively all packaged foods regulated by the FDA had to include a nutrition label [4].

The NLEA also established important terminology that we still find today. Previous to the NLEA, there was no established standard as to what labeling jargon such as "low", "reduced", or "free" meant [3]. For example, a package labeled "low in sodium" could have represented a low overall sodium content or it could have simply meant lower sodium than the previous version of the same product. Clearly, such inconsistent terminology could be quite confusing for consumers in terms of making healthy decisions. The NLEA proceeded to establish specific requirements that had to be met in order for a manufacturer to include such terminology on their packaging. For example, as outlined in the FDA's "Code of Federal Regulations" (CFR), food packaging that uses terms that represent a lack of sodium in the product such as "sodium free" "zero sodium" or "no sodium" require that the following conditions are met for that product [3]:

> 1) *The food item must contain less than five milligrams (mg) of sodium per serving,*
> 2) *The food does not contain salt in the ingredients or is thought by consumers to contain sodium, and*
> 3) *The food, normally included without the benefit of special processing or alteration is labeled to disclose that sodium is not usually present in the food (e.g., "leaf lettuce, a sodium-free food")*

Other sodium-specific claims such as "very low sodium", "low sodium", or "reduced sodium" each have their own set of conditions that must be met in order to include the claim on the packaging label. Furthermore, the CFR separates sodium claims from salt claims, such that labeling a food a "unsalted" does not necessarily allow it to be labeled as "sodium free" unless it meets the requirements of a sodium-free product. While these guidelines may seem quite rigorous, they serve to help protect you the consumer and ensure that there is consistency across the industry. After all, mislabeling a product's sodium content could have significant and detrimental consequences for those of us who are sensitive to sodium fluctuations in our body.

Determining sodium content

Nutrition labels tell us as consumers how much sodium is in a serving size of a certain food item. To determine sodium content, one of two approaches will be used. The first approach is to determine the sodium content of the 'finished food', which outlines the amount of sodium present in the food's prepared state. For this analysis, a portion of a particular food product is processed and analyzed in its final form by putting it through a series of chemical tests (more on that later) that ultimately reveals the sodium content of that portion of food. Say, for example, a fast food establishment develops a new double-meat sandwich with a 'special sauce'. To determine a food's sodium content (along with all other nutrients) using the analysis process, the sandwich is prepared as if it were being served to a customer and then ground up. A small sample of a known proportion (say 100 grams, for example) is then analyzed and the sodium amount in that sample is determined. Then, the final sodium amount of the food item is calculated by multiplying out the amount of sodium in the sample by that amount contained in the entire sandwich in order to establish the sodium content of the entire sandwich. In other words, if a 10-gram sample of the sandwich had 7 milligrams of sodium, and if the prepared sandwich weighs 400 grams, then the prepared sandwich would be estimated to have 280mg of sodium (7mg * 40).

Using the chemical analysis method to determine sodium content ensures that all ingredients in the food are analyzed in the amount at which they are consumed. It is important to note that with chemical analysis, the final analysis is specific to a single order or 'preparation' of that food item. What that means is that if a recipe is later altered, or if someone else prepares the same food item differently, the analyzed sodium content may be somewhat different from what is actually served. For example, if a restaurant chain has a seafood platter analyzed and one teaspoon (equivalent to two shakes of the seasoning canister in the restaurant's kitchen) of the seasoning mix was included in the preparation sent for analysis, it may provide a final value of say 1200mg of sodium. But, if in the actual restaurant four shakes were added by the cook on duty that day, the consumed food may end up with 2000mg of sodium.

Chemically analyzing sodium content

In addition to the FDA's requirement that a food nutrition label be added to packaged food, it can also impart a significant cost for the food manufacturer – up to $2000 per food item [2], depending on the options requested. For us on a low-sodium diet, the most meaningful output of this analysis is obviously the sodium content. But how exactly is the sodium content of a particular food item determined?

At present, there are four predominant methods used to determine the sodium content of a food sample, each of which can be used to reliably estimate the sodium content of a food item. The method used is typically up to the individual analytical lab, with factors such as cost, reliability, ease of use, and accuracy/precision influencing the analytical test used.

The first method, electric conductivity, takes advantage of the fact that sodium chloride separates into separate sodium and chloride ions when in a solution such as water [6]. The individual charges of these electrons influence the conductivity of a liquid containing the ions, and this conductivity can be measured. With "amperometric" probes, the electrical current along with the resistance between two electrodes can be measured, and the resulting value can be used to calculate the presence of sodium in a specific amount of liquid. Similarly, "potentiometric" probes send a current into a liquid while additional probes detect how much the known voltage is altered by the liquid. The change in known versus altered current values can reveal the sodium present in a liquid.

A second method for analyzing sodium content is refractometry, which analyzes how well light travels through a material, in this case a solution containing sodium [5]. Mechanical refractometry involves placing a sample on one end of a hollow tool that resembles a miniature telescope and then looking through the other end. The degree of refraction of light passing through the refractometer is proportional to the amount of sodium in the sample. Digital refractometers are also available, and are generally more accurate.

The third option for analyzing a food's sodium content is the use of ion-sensitive electrodes [5, 6]. This technique utilizes a chemical sensor that is enclosed within a probe to determine the concentration of sodium ions in a liquid. A membrane on the probe and the sensor produce a voltage proportional to the amount of sodium present.

Another method for assessing sodium content is termed titration [5, 6]. With titration, a particular liquid such as silver nitrate is added to the sodium-containing liquid. When silver nitrate is added in excess of what is needed, the excess binds with another ion and produces a red color, signifying that all sodium has been accounted for. The sodium content can then be determined off of the amount of silver nitrate liquid that was added prior to the sodium-containing liquid turning a red color.

Despite what you may think after watching some legal-drama television show, determining sodium content is not as simple as tearing off a piece of hamburger and dropping it into a liquid. Rather, the sample used for sodium analysis must first be prepared. This usually consists of placing a food sample into a liquid and then homogenizing, or 'crushing' the food sample into the smallest bits possible. This releases the sodium into the liquid, creating a solution. To separate the remaining food particles – which will affect the analysis if not removed – from the liquid, the container is then spun at a very high speed in a centrifuge which then forces the larger food particles to the bottom of the container while the sodium remains suspended in the solution, which is then withdrawn from the container and used for the actual analysis.

Ingredient-based sodium analysis

In addition to chemical analysis, another option for measuring a food's sodium content – and one that is much more viable for consumers – is the ingredient-based sodium analysis. This method determines a food's nutrition content by adding up the nutrition values of the individual ingredients used to make up the food. For example, sodium analysis for a corn dog recipe would require adding up the previously-calculated sodium content of both the hot dog and all of the components of the batter to reach a final sodium content for a particular serving size. Using this method also requires that the serving size is established. If, for example, a serving size of the corndog is equal to 'one corndog', the sodium content is determined based on all ingredients required to make one corndog. This might be calculated as the sodium content of one hotdog plus the sodium contained in ¼ cup of batter. However, it is necessary to sum up the sodium content of each ingredient used in the batter, also. Therefore, the sodium content of one corndog is equivalent to the sodium content of the ingredients in each hotdog, plus the sodium content of all ingredients used to make ¼ cup of batter. This final total would be the amount listed on the corndog's nutrition label.

It's important to understand that what goes into a recipe is not always what comes out, especially in terms of sodium. For example, in developing a hamburger patty you would record the sodium content of the ground beef (or whatever meat you start with) as well as the remaining ingredients and spices. However, by the time the meat cooks, much of the fat has dripped off, and may carry with it some of the sodium. Similarly, consuming only the green beans in a can – and not any of the liquid – should be expected to result in a lower sodium consumption than what is on the label. Each of these examples would reduce the sodium content of the finished product versus the ingredient-based method. Similarly, a meat-based recipe which calls for a marinating liquid typically results in a large amount of liquid ingredients just for the marinade. However, only a small amount of marinade makes it into the meat for cooking while the majority of the marinade is poured off. Using the ingredient-based method would artificially inflate your recipe's sodium content due to the excess, unconsumed marinade.

Let's look at a practical example which will highlight how the ingredient-based method is not always best for determining sodium content. Take a recipe that calls for ¼ cup of soy sauce to be added to a marinade – that soy sauce in itself would easily contribute 2000mg or more of sodium to the recipe nutrition. However, if only one teaspoon of that soy sauce actually adheres to the meat and makes it to the consumption stage, only 300mg or so would be in the final prepared recipe – a much more acceptable amount for the low-sodium consumer. Furthermore, if the marinade liquid – along with the embedded sodium – drips off the meat during the cooking process, the finished food would be expected to have even less sodium. So while the ingredient-based method is rather simple and has little associated cost up front, the 'finished food' chemical-based analysis could be considered more accurate in that it only counts that sodium remaining in the meat after the meat has been cooked. Therefore, the finished food's sodium should be expected to be just a fraction of the initial ingredient-based sodium content.

Regardless of the method used, both analysis methods will give you a final sodium result based on either an analyzed sodium composition or a summed total of ingredients. In either case, it should be expected that the sodium value calculated is accurate, though the ingredient-based method will largely be accurate only to the point that the original ingredients remained in the food. Still, as we'll discuss in Chapter 7, once you begin to cook your own foods you will likely become quite familiar with the ingredient-based method as you will be relying on several nutrition labels to total up your sodium consumption.

Determining sodium content from the food label

The food nutrition label (now called the "Nutrition Facts" label) itself has changed over the years before arriving at its present state [3]. These changes have resulted from research over time using various input from focus groups, consumer trends, and changes in the recommended nutrition intake. The label may be somewhat daunting at first sight, but for an individual adhering to a low sodium diet, there are only two or maybe three main aspects that you need to be aware of. By understanding these components of the nutrition label you can easily and accurately calculate the sodium content of the food product you are consuming, which will better allow you to track your daily sodium consumption.

On the nutrition label (Figure 6.1), sodium will be expressed in milligrams (1/1000th of a gram). On the right side of the label, on the "sodium" line, you will see a number with a percentage (%) sign. This represents the percent of the recommended daily sodium intake each serving provides. To me, this percentage number has no value and I generally ignore it. Why? Because the recommended intake percentage is based on a 2,300mg (i.e. 1 teaspoon) sodium intake – much higher than my personal targeted goal of 1000mg daily.

The first and most important section of the food label that I will look at is the food's listed sodium content. Why? Because that number gives me a quick representation of total sodium content. If the sodium content on that line is high (for

Nutrition Facts
Serving Size 5 oz. (120g)
Servings Per Container 4

Amount Per Serving

| Calories | 33 |
| Calories from Fat | 0 |

	% Daily Value*
Total Fat 0g	
Saturated Fat 0g	0%
Cholesterol 0mg	0%
Sodium 25mg	0%
Total Carbohydrate 16g	1%
Dietary Fiber 0g	5%
Sugars 1g	0%
Protein 2g	

| Vitamin A 180% | • | Vitamin C 15% |
| Calcium 5% | • | Iron 2% |

Percent Daily Values are based on a 2,000 calorie diet. Your daily values may be higher or lower depending on your calorie needs.

		Calories	2,000	2,500
Total Fat	Less Than		65g	80g
Sat Fat	Less Than		20g	25g
Cholesterol	Less Than		300mg	300mg
Sodium	Less Than		2,400 mg	2,400mg
Total Carbohydrate			300g	375g
Dietary Fiber			25g	30g

Figure 6.1. A standard Nutrition Facts label. Note the areas we discuss, including the serving size, servings per container, and sodium content per serving.

me, 300mg or more per serving is considered 'high'), it indicates to me that I won't get much benefit out of that food as there will be a significant sodium risk in consuming it. We will talk shortly about the serving size, of which the sodium value represents. If the listed sodium value (per serving) is high, then eating a more realistic portion (i.e. several servings

138

for me, in most cases) will just contribute an additional high amount of sodium. Similarly, if the sodium content is quite low on the label but there is also a very small serving size (e.g. 1 tsp), such as occurs in foods like salsa – of which I tend to need quite a bit to feel 'full' – the trade-off isn't really worth the sodium risk.

Sodium content means nothing without putting that sodium amount into context. In other words, how much food must be consumed in order to intake the amount of sodium listed on the Nutrition Facts label? For example, if a food label lists the amount of sodium as 470mg, is that sodium amount what I would consume if I ate the entire food item or just 1/10th of the food item? Whatever sodium amount you find on the label – whether it be 10mg in a package of corn tortillas or 1,200mg on the side of a can of soup – that amount only represents the sodium contained in each serving. Therefore, you next have to look at the serving size near the top of the label in order to understand what portion of the food contains the listed sodium amount. If the corn tortilla package indicates that the sodium content is 10mg and the Nutrition Facts label outlines that one serving equals one corn tortilla, then eating one corn tortilla means that you would will consume 10mg of sodium.

Remember earlier when I said that there were 'maybe three' parts of the Nutrition Facts label to pay attention to? We are now ready to discuss that third part, as it is related to the serving size. Before we get started, go ahead and grab a soft drink – preferably a can or bottle. Not to drink, but to show you just how misleading Nutrition Facts labels can be unless

139

you take into context that third component – "servings per container". If I look at a particular brand's 12-ounce can of diet soda, alongside its 20-ounce sibling, I see that both labels list a serving size as "one can" or "one bottle" even though the size of each container is different. So, according to the label if I drink either 12 ounces or 20 ounces of diet soda, I've consumed one serving – despite the eight ounces of difference between the two. In theory this makes sense, as most everyone consumes one can or one bottle of soda once it has been opened. However, according to the Nutrition label on each, for the 12 ounce can I have consumed 40mg of sodium, while drinking the 20-ounce bottle provides 70mg of sodium. This difference illustrates that it is important to also look at how many *servings per container* exist if you intend to consume the entire container. Look at a standard-sized can of green beans, for example. Though it may not seem like much of a meal, each can contains 3.5 servings given that one serving is equivalent to just ½ cup. Why is that so important? Because the Nutrition Facts label from a 14.5 ounce can of green beans shows a serving size as ½ cup and 380mg of sodium per serving, and if you mistakenly thought that the whole can equaled one serving (as it does when dealing with soft drinks) you would actually be consuming 1,330mg of sodium! Similarly, most breads have a serving size of *one slice.* If you really think about it, how many people do you know that consume a single slice of bread per sitting?

Speaking of serving sizes – just who determines how much food makes up one serving? Well, in a roundabout way – we all do. The serving size listed on a nutrition facts label comes from survey data that consumers completed many years ago, resulting in what is called the "Reference Amount Customarily Consumed", or "RACC" [10]. Those surveys provided data to manufacturers regarding how much of a food item an average consumer reported eating at one sitting. While these serving sizes provide a set amount by which to base sodium content on, they are not exactly 'one size fits all'. This can be somewhat problematic for those of us on a low-sodium diet when it comes to the sodium content of our food. In particular, those like me who are a little bigger than the average consumer and who tend to eat a bit more at each meal must be especially careful of monitoring nutrition labels in order to ensure that we are properly calculating our sodium intake.

This brings up an additional confusing principle – just how much of what we eat equals a serving size? If I sprinkle on some shredded cheese to my taco, and a serving size of shredded cheese is ¼ cup, how do I calculate total sodium content based on a 'sprinkle'? There is no easy way to answer this other than to actually measure out one time (in cups or in weight) what you would normally add, and then base all future uses of food like shredded cheese off of this amount. Understand that you will never be perfect in your total sodium milligram amount, but you should end up close enough that it won't impact your health.

The somewhat randomness of the serving sizes is particularly important if you are using a computer program to tally your sodium intake, especially if you select "one serving" or some other pre-determined value. If the program utilizes the sodium content in a 12-ounce serving and you actually consumed one 20-ounce serving, you will be off by 35mg of sodium for each 20-ounce diet soft drink you consume that day. While perhaps not a health-altering amount on its own, if this occurs across multiple food types specific to sodium consumption, you could ultimately be eating a much higher level of sodium than you had planned. To help avoid this, ensure that when using a computer-based nutrition log you are entering the actual serving size (i.e. "8 ounces") rather than using a default amount such as "1 serving".

What does all of this mean? Quite frankly, it means that as a sodium-conscious consumer you will need to be diligent about noting the sodium content per serving and the serving size, and also be sure to pay attention to the servings per container. Again, if you drink one bottle of soft drink you have consumed 70mg of sodium. However, if you are not careful and apply that same rationale of consuming the entire container's worth to, say, a can of soup, you could get yourself into some serious sodium trouble. The Nutrition Facts on a can of soup lists 870mg of sodium per serving. If you were to assume that one serving equals one can (instead of the listed 2.5 servings per can), you will unwittingly consume 2,175mg of sodium! Instead, you will need to be sure that if 870mg is allowable on your daily sodium intake, you must only consume 40% of the can. Or, you will need to account for 2,175mg of sodium if you choose to consume the entire can.

Sodium in the ingredients

What we have discussed so far is directed at the sodium content of prepared foods themselves, many of which require no additional ingredients for the food to be cooked to its final state. Things change significantly if a pre-packaged food requires additional ingredients which can themselves contain sodium. This then magnifies the sodium content of that food's nutrition label and complicates the procedure for calculating total sodium content. This is common in many dry products which require the addition of wet materials such as milk or broth, as each contain sodium and therefore contribute further to the total sodium content of a prepared food product.

Let's take an easy one – cereal. No one I know prefers to eat cereal plain, straight out of the box. And few – if any – people I know only eat the actual serving size of ¾ - 1 cup. Rather, they eat about 1.5 – 2 cups and add milk to it. So, if we took a popular cereal with its 140mg/cup, and assume that 1.5 cups were eaten, it would provide 210mg of sodium. But, if one cup (8oz) of whole milk was also added, another 120mg of sodium would need to be factored in when logging your sodium content for 'cereal'. Similarly, did you remember to factor in how much ketchup and/or mustard was consumed with the aforementioned corn dog. In other words, the *total* amount of sodium must be accounted for from all components of a consumed food in order to properly determine the meal's sodium content. You must be sure to account for the sodium, serving size, and the amount used for *each* required ingredient of a packaged food, particularly if additional ingredients are required during the food's preparation.

So why is it that packaged foods contain such a high sodium content? The most blatant answer lies in what we covered in Chapter 5 – food preservation and flavoring. As we discussed, most wet foods – such as canned vegetables – are going to spoil relatively quickly on the shelf if left in their original state. A short shelf life increases the risk that a food product doesn't make it to the checkout line – so sodium chloride is often added to increase the shelf life. But even dry packaged foods – take ramen noodles as an example – spoil very slowly but are still very high in sodium. Why? Those foods – the type that often include 'flavor packets' – are often packed with sodium chloride in order to enhance flavor. How much salt or sodium is added? The official answer is revealed in the sodium content per serving, multiplied by the number of servings per container. However, another answer to that question is revealed in the rules regarding the order of ingredients as listed on the package label.

The FDA mandates that the ingredients list, usually found directly underneath the Nutrition Facts label, be listed in descending order by weight [9]. What that means is that the ingredient in the food product that weighs the most must be listed first, the ingredient that weighs second-most must be listed second, and so on until the ingredient with the least weight (usually spices) is listed last. For example, a simple can of traditional green beans may have an ingredients list of "green beans, water, and salt". All you can infer from that ingredient list is that the green beans and the water weigh more than the salt. However, the ingredient order doesn't list the content, only the order of the ingredients by total weight.

Interestingly, I have found that the ingredient list doesn't always match well with what the nutrition facts label shows. I still have an unused three-ounce container of kettle corn popcorn seasoning that lists the sodium content as 0mg per serving. Upon seeing that, I was compelled to buy it as I love a big bowl of popcorn, and now it appeared as though I had an opportunity to enjoy it with a bit of sweet and buttery topping. However, upon later looking at the ingredients list I found that it included "sugar, salt, natural flavors, silicon dioxide". The contrast between the Nutrition Facts label's sodium content and the ingredient list indicating salt as the second ingredient was very confusing – so much that I called the manufacturer. Their response was that there probably wasn't enough sodium in the container to even register in the analysis! Personally, I have a high degree of doubt that with salt listed as 2nd on the ingredient list that there is enough to outweigh two ingredients but still not show up in the analysis.

Carefully analyzing the ingredient list is important as it helps you determine the source of the sodium in the food product. As we explored in Chapter 5, there are several sources for sodium, including table salt. One way that manufacturers can reduce the appearance of salt is to include the word "seasonings" on the ingredient label and then in parentheses listing out what those seasonings are. You might see this occur in foods that included prepared items like pasta – the pasta ingredients will be listed out first – followed by additional ingredients such as those in the seasoning packet. In reality, salt may be very high up on the ingredient list but it is lost in the long list of ingredients.

For example, a brand of ramen noodles claiming 500mg of sodium per package lists out the six noodle ingredients, followed by the oil used for cooking the noodles, then salt, followed by twenty-seven additional ingredients. So when following the rules for the ingredient list you would be correct in saying that there is more salt in the ramen noodle package than 27 other ingredients. However, after the mention of salt the ingredient list also states that the product is comprised of less than 2% of the remaining 27 ingredients. In other words, salt is evidently at *least* two percent of the food by weight. Ironically, of those 27 remaining ingredients in the ramen noodle package, several are sodium based: disodium guanylate, disodium inosinate, disodium succinate, sodium alginate, sodium carbonate, and sodium tripolyphosphate. I would venture to guess that most of those sodium-based ingredients can be found in the separate seasoning packet enclosed with the noodles. In the next chapter we will discuss how to still enjoy foods such as ramen noodles that have these high-sodium flavor packets without consuming the high amount of sodium listed on the package label.

Sodium in menu items

Up to this point we have talked about packaged foods such as canned vegetables, ramen noodles, and cereal. Now, let's take a look at the sodium content of prepared foods such as what you would find in a fast food joint or a restaurant.

Enter cautiously though - if you think horror novels are frightening, taking a close look at the nutrition charts at some of your favorite restaurants may leave you equally shocked. What exactly is a nutrition chart, you may ask? It's basically a "Nutrition Facts" for dishes and food items you can order off the menu at a restaurant. The Federal Food, Drug, and Cosmetic Act of 2009 requires that chain restaurants that have 20 or more separate locations must list the number of calories, the total grams of saturated fat, trans fat, and carbohydrates, and the total milligrams of sodium [7]. This is a major step up, as before this Act there were no requirements for sodium labeling on restaurant products despite decades of requiring the sodium content to be listed on store-bought products. Requiring the nutrition chart has made life much simpler for the low-sodium consumer, especially in the realm of being able to enjoy restaurant food.

These days, most all big-box restaurants provide their nutrition charts either on the wall at the restaurant or make them available online. By paying close attention to these nutrition charts you can often enjoy whole meals with little worry about sodium content, as you can calculate total sodium content of individual foods and then build a meal out of those lower-sodium food items (e.g. salad, plain burger, and a dessert). It would serve you well to look up a restaurant's nutrition chart online before you head there to eat, as understanding the sodium content of the food you are ordering will make you a more-informed consumer and may influence your likelihood of eating there. For example, a simple online search reveals that at many seafood restaurants, the listed total

147

sodium content in several dishes can exceed 4000mg, with most entrées exceeding 2000mg. If you choose to patronize the restaurant, it may be difficult for the restaurant to get any reduction in those sodium amounts as the food may be shipped pre-seasoned. Therefore, you may be better off assembling a group of low-sodium side dishes or simply having a salad.

In my experience, venturing into the land of restaurant dining often lands us low-sodium people in quite a quandary – either find a restaurant with low-sodium options that has a menu that everyone likes, or find a restaurant that everyone likes and hope you can find a way to create your own low-sodium options.

One thing that is nice about restaurant nutrition charts is that the sodium values are almost always representative of the total sodium content for the entire food item rather than for a serving size. In other words, the nutrition chart will show the sodium content for the entire order of French fries rather than "8 ounces" of fries, as you might find on a Nutrition Facts label's listed serving size. This makes calculating the total sodium consumed much easier than multiplying sodium content by serving size as you will have to do often when using Nutrition Facts labels in your kitchen.

Because we are discussing restaurants, it's relevant to rehash a point we made earlier regarding the nutrition chart's listed sodium content. Remember that if the dish was sent off for analysis of sodium content, it does not mean that every subsequently-prepared dish will have the same sodium content as what is listed on the chart. I would venture to guess that any dish sent off for analysis had very stringent control over its ingredients, as I doubt that there was any additional salt or other ingredients added to a dish whose nutrition (such as calories, fat, etc.) would be chemically revealed. Instead, you should take into account the individuality of each restaurant and each kitchen worker/chef that prepares your meal. Therefore, I always personally add an additional 20% or so to the listed sodium amount in order to make up for individual variation in the dish's preparation at that particular restaurant. Unfortunately, this added amount can sometimes push a dish's sodium content beyond my own personal 'acceptable limit' of sodium, but I'd rather be safe than take the risk of consuming some unexpected amount of sodium.

Before you go to any restaurant – accept this truth: restaurants are for the most part NOT sodium conscious. Whereas the majority of consumers are also not sodium conscious, restaurants don't have an inherent need to cater to a very small portion of their clientele. Salt is generally perceived to improve flavor, and restaurants want to enhance their food's flavor in order to bring in more customers. This means that rarely will you find a restaurant where you can go and eat what you want off of the menu without concern. In my own little fantasy world it's my hope that this book may help make that a reality – a 'low sodium' restaurant where people like us can enjoy the menu rather than just limiting ourselves to partaking in a few particular menu items. I would love to consistently see a "low sodium" section of the menu just like you will find a "gluten free" or "heart healthy" section. But much like how there used to be wide variation on food labels as to what 'low sodium' meant, it is equally true that restaurants have a wide variation in what low-sodium means to them. A dish being reduced in sodium from 3700mg to 1900mg might be considered low-sodium compared to the original recipe, but the total sodium content is still extremely high for individuals trying to stay low-sodium. Until universal low-sodium menu guidelines are established, we're stuck with what exists currently – mostly high-sodium menu choices with minimal options for generating a low-sodium version when we decide to eat out. The menu focus seems to still be on calories, but with the recent inclusion of gluten-free items perhaps us sodium-wary folks won't have to wait much longer.

References

1. (1969). "White House Conference on Food, Nutrition, and Health, December 2-4, 1969, Washington, D. C." The Journal of Infectious Diseases **120**(5): 637-641.

2. Agricultural Research Service (2017). Nutrient Data Laboratory. U. S. D. o. Agriculture.

3. Boon, C. S., et al. (2010). Front-of-package Nutrition Rating Systems and Symbols: Phase I Report, National Academies Press.

4. Marietta, A. B., et al. (1999). "Knowledge, attitudes, and behaviors of college students regarding the 1990 Nutrition Labeling Education Act food labels." **99**(4): 445-449.

5. Masulli, D. (2015). "Determining Salt in Food." 2019, from https://www.foodqualityandsafety.com/article/determining-salt-in-food/?singlepage=1.

6. Nielsen, S. (2015). Sodium Determination Using Ion Selective Electrodes, Mohr Titration, and Test Strips. Food Analysis Laboratory Manual. USA, Springer.

7.   United States Department of Health and Human Services (2014). Food Labeling: Nutrition Labeling of Standard Menu Items in Restaurants and Similar Retail Food Establishments. F. a. D. Administration.

8.   United States Food and Drug Administration (1998). Guidance for Industry: Nutrition Labeling Manual - A Guide for Developing and Using Data Bases. U. S. D. o. H. a. H. Services.

9.   United States Food and Drug Administration (2013). A Food Labeling Guide: Guidance For Industry.

10.   United States Food and Drug Administration (2016). Food Labeling: Serving Sizes of Foods that Can Reasonably Be Consumed at One Eating Occasion; Dual-Column Labeling; Updating, Modifying, and Establishing Certain Reference Amounts Customarily Consumed; Serving Size for Breath Mints; and Technical Amendments.

Chapter 7 - Reducing sodium in your diet

So here we are – the final chapter in a book about helping you to understand the basics involved in living a low-sodium life. Take a minute and reflect on what all you have learned up to this point. You now have a better understanding of sodium as an element and ion, as well as the various types of sodium compounds. You have a clear understanding of sodium's role in the body and how your body captures sodium's unique properties in order to perform normal functions that we all take for granted. You have reviewed several medical conditions related to sodium and understand how sodium influences these conditions. You better understand how the food industry takes advantage of sodium's properties in order to prepare food products. And, you have learned how to analyze a nutrition label in order to take control of your sodium intake.

So what's left? Perhaps the most important part – a better understanding of how to reduce your daily sodium intake and still enjoy eating great food! You might be wondering why I waited until getting seven chapters in before covering this area. The reason is that I personally believe you will better grasp the material now towards the end of the book since you have a firm foundation regarding the topics we covered earlier in the book. That foundation has helped you develop a rationale for why you should try to limit your sodium, and now it's time to discuss some techniques that will assist you in lowering your sodium intake.

In this chapter, I'll outline several tricks and techniques I have found over time that you can use to help get your sodium intake levels down. Using these techniques will allow you to enjoy foods without sacrificing a large portion of your diet that you may have felt were inaccessible on a low sodium diet. For example, soups were off my personal menu early on. Over time though, I discovered a variety of ingredient substitutions that now allow me to enjoy many different soups. Whereas you can also implement over time many of the tips and tricks we'll discuss in this chapter, it can help you develop a low-sodium mindset that can assist you in making smarter food decisions about sodium. Because eating out can provide unique challenges compared to eating at home, we'll separate the topics into three food settings: tips and techniques for the home, tips for eating out, and tips for when you are at social gatherings that aren't quite a formal setting but may present unique challenges to sticking to your low-sodium commitment.

Remember these points

Before we dig into the core of what this chapter is about – ways to reduce your sodium intake – there are a few important points about being successful in the low sodium lifestyle that we need to emphasize. Point number one:

establish and stick to your personalized daily sodium intake allowance. For some of us, a daily sodium limit was likely established by our personal physician. Others may have developed their sodium limit over time by learning that a certain level of sodium intake sets off cues within their body. For me, I was never given any instructions other than to 'reduce my sodium'. Over the years, though, I have learned that a 1000mg daily total keeps me pretty much symptom-free. You may be at a higher or lower level.

Let's focus on this daily sodium level for a moment. I like to think of my own daily sodium limit as my allowable "sodium budget", which similar to a spending budget is the amount of sodium I allow myself to eat per day. Throughout the day, those foods that I eat draw me closer to my sodium budget maximum, while sweaty exercise moves me away from my sodium budget total since exercise removes sodium from my system. It is the balance of these two activities (eating and exercising) that largely dictate what I eat each day, for if I go for a long, sweaty run I may allow myself a higher-sodium meal later in the day. When it comes down to it, your sodium budget operates much like how your income versus your required expenditures might guide what you purchase each day.

If you follow a similar format as me and also treat your sodium budget akin to a financial budget, I will give you one particular caveat in that I wouldn't recommend 'saving' your sodium throughout your day and then using it all at once at dinner in the same fashion you may save up money and then purchase a large item. Using all of your daily sodium budget at once would in effect shock your system by sending a large amount of sodium into your body all at once, likely negating the effect of maintaining a steady, healthy sodium level in your body. A sudden surge in your body's sodium level can be problematic for conditions such as Ménière's disease that are thought to be affected by rapid changes in sodium levels [1]. Rather than saving your sodium up for a later high-sodium meal, I recommend that you make an effort to spread out your sodium budget across the entire day, and consider establishing per-meal sodium allowances (e.g. 300mg for breakfast, 500mg for lunch, etc.) that match up with your daily intake goals and will can help guide your food choices and ensure that you maintain a path to your sodium goals.

Just like running your own financial budget, creating a sodium budget can make you more aware of your food choices and keep you on track to stay within your target sodium budget each day. For me, my daily sodium budget dictates my food choices. In fact, the biggest factor that helps me keep my sodium budget in check is point number two for this chapter: consider a food's sodium content in relation to the amount of food involved. In other words, I evaluate a food item's bulk-to-sodium ratio. We hit on this concept briefly in the previous chapter when we analyzed both sodium content per serving and the serving size when determining how much sodium is in a particular container of food. By looking at a food's bulk-to-sodium ratio, it can help us determine whether eating a certain food item makes common sense based on its sodium content.

Allow me to explain a little better. When considering a snack, food item, or meal, a primary question I will ask myself is *what amount of food will I get in return for a specific hit on my sodium budget*? For example, if it's lunch time and I want to stick to, say, a 300mg sodium limit for the meal (keeping my 1000mg daily budget in mind), I will certainly not choose a lunch that includes 10 seasoned crackers containing 325mg of sodium. Doing so would use up almost 1/3 of my sodium budget with just the 10 crackers, and those crackers will certainly not curb my hunger enough to hold me over until dinner. In fact, if I did eat the crackers and consumed my allowable sodium level for that meal, I would be guaranteed to be hungry again very soon afterwards. This would in turn make it very likely that I would consume additional food later on, which will likely also contain some degree of additional sodium. Therefore, my decision would no doubt be to pass on the crackers as a lunch choice, as the bulk amount of food (10 crackers) is not worth the sodium cost (325mg, or 1/3 of my daily budget).

Instead of the crackers, I would look for a food item that has a better bulk-to-sodium ratio that would be more likely to fill me up for the same relative cost to my sodium budget. For example, three servings of my home-cooked fried rice might deliver me 280mg of sodium, but the amount of food I get for that 280mg of sodium is enough to fill me up. Therefore, being full after eating three servings of a meal containing 280mg of sodium is a much more logical option than eating a smaller quantity of food (such as 10 crackers) containing 325mg of food and still being hungry. This bulk-to-sodium ratio drives many of the food decisions I make, including what to eat for a snack. Developing your own similar system is something that I recommend you consider, as it can help keep you aware of food choices relative to your sodium intake and may help prevent those small, incremental intakes of sodium that can come from additional snacking fits when you aren't quite full after a meal.

A final point – point number three – is to understand that adhering to a low-sodium diet is a lifestyle change. It is not a temporary plan. As I mentioned earlier, your old way of carefree menu ordering and late night fast-food pickups won't work in a low-sodium world. In fact, while cheating on a weight-loss diet can result in a pound or two of weight gain, cheating on your low-sodium diet may have medical complications. Therefore, you must accept the fact that becoming a low-sodium consumer will require you to develop a new mindset regarding the foods you eat as well as the way you eat. You will have to give up certain convenience foods that you used to enjoy in their traditional form – fast food and restaurant entrees, sausages and cured meats, boxed dinners, canned soups, and other classically high-sodium foods. Does this mean that you cannot enjoy some of those foods? Certainly not. I still love to eat sausage, I eat various soups four or five times a month, and still order restaurant French fries, steaks, and entrees when eating out. I even enjoy handfuls of beef jerky! The difference between the degree of success and enjoyment of your new low-sodium life versus how you used to eat lies in the preparation of those foods, as eating foods straight out of the box or off of the menu just isn't going to be feasible for you in today's high-sodium food industry. Rather, you'll need to start investigating ways to make foods at home, or how to build a low-sodium meal off of existing menu items.

Enjoying delicious prepared foods is still a certainty - it just takes a little extra preparation on your part. And that's what we're going to discuss next.

Reducing your sodium intake in the home

When it comes to the food we eat, it isn't rocket science to understand that the food is either prepared fresh by us at home, prepared from a store-bought mix at home, or prepared by someone else when we eat out. If the latter scenarios relate to you and you want to adhere to a low-sodium lifestyle, don't worry – it's possible. Understand though that you will be taking some degree of inherent risk every time someone else prepares your food, specifically that risk of whether the actual sodium content matches what you *think* is in the food. At home we have a relatively solid level of control over our food since we see what specifically is going into each dish. You hold the boxes, you analyze the nutrition labels, and you read the ingredients. Allowing someone else to prepare your food, though, removes this level of control. For example, you may have told the waiter to make sure there was no added salt, but did she remember to tell the chef? Or, did the chef withhold the seasoning from the wrong entree? While eating out or being at a social gathering with friends is nice, restaurant waiters, fast food attendants, and even our close friends cannot be expected to understand the intricacies of just what "low sodium" entails, and therefore may only know to 'hold the seasoning' without also knowing if the ingredients themselves are also salted. Whereas you will likely be eating a significant portion of food at home while on your new low-sodium adventure, we'll first outline ways you can reduce sodium intake in the controlled setting of your home. Even if you're not experienced in the kitchen, don't worry – it's fun, and if you're like me you'll take pride in knowing exactly what your family is consuming.

Look for lower-sodium options

Before you can make your meal, you have to have the right ingredients. Finding those ingredients requires making informed shopping decisions. We talked earlier about food labels and how labeling can list foods as sodium-free, low-sodium, or 'no salt added'. Because of the trend towards becoming a more health-conscious society, these labeling guidelines have made it easier as a shopper to immediately recognize a food's sodium content and thereby improve our ability to find foods that have a lower sodium content. With no noticeable sacrifice in taste and no real difference in price, these reduced-sodium items open up a wealth of recipes and food options which we can enjoy without worrying about the impact on our sodium budget.

Take, for example, the changes that have occurred in canned foods. When you are preparing a meal that requires a type of canned food, several options that previously would not have been affordable on your daily sodium budget are now allowable due to the "no salt added" (NSA) option. Canned corn, beans, tomatoes, tomato sauce, and many other canned foods packaged under the 'no salt added' label contain just a fraction of the sodium (e.g. 20mg per serving) of their regularly-packed siblings (380mg per serving). Quite frankly, I'm not quite sure why the regular-sodium options even exist anymore – I nor any of my family or guests have reported any difference in taste, and shelf life between the regular and no-salt-added option is effectively the same in terms of expiration dates. One potential problem with NSA-based canned foods is that you will typically find these foods only at supermarkets. I've had difficulty finding *any* NSA canned food at a convenience store or small-town grocer. Hopefully this changes in the future, but for now, finding the best low-sodium foods may add a few miles to your shopping trip.

Even though NSA canned foods provide a great option, I recommend you always strive to use fresh, natural ingredients first. Fresh carrots, green beans, tomatoes and other vegetables are often just as cost-effective as their canned siblings but with a much lower sodium content. For me, finding recipes that are heavy on meat or vegetables are favorites as I know that when I throw in some rice or pasta I can easily create a low-sodium meal for the whole family. Finding fully compliant recipes can take some effort though, as there have been many, many times that I've found a great-sounding recipe online only to be deterred by ingredients like "cream of mushroom soup", or "ranch dressing packet". Therefore, focus on looking for those recipes that can be created with as many naturally low-sodium ingredients as possible, including vegetables, meats, pastas, rice, and dairy. Ingredients which are packaged with preservatives such as sodium chloride or include seasonings will only serve to increase the meal's sodium content.

While canned NSA foods are a staple in our house, making my own baked goods became an option once I found sodium-free baking powder. Items like cakes, quick breads, holiday cookies, and even biscuits are now on the menu as a result. While you can find a sodium-free baking soda online, I just use twice the amount of sodium-free baking powder as what the recipe originally called for with baking soda. For example, if a biscuit recipe calls for ½ teaspoon of baking soda, I will instead add 1 teaspoon of sodium-free baking powder. Personally, I have yet to have a recipe malfunction using this substitution. There has been online discussions about substituting baking powder for baking soda in that it is reported to influence the taste, but I haven't found that to be an issue.

Seasonings have low-sodium and sodium-free options too!

While foods such as canned vegetables have made major strides in terms of low-sodium options, most packaged dinner meals you find on store shelves have not. Often, these packaged foods contain a major enemy in the world of the low-sodium consumer – the infamous seasoning packet. We talked in the previous chapter about some of the ingredients that can be found in these packets – such as are included with ramen noodles, which can themselves consist of several forms of sodium. This same seasoning packet is likely providing 90% or more of the sodium content of the associated food. How is it

162

then that I frequently enjoy store-bought ramen noodles yet still end up adding almost no sodium to my sodium budget? Simple – I substitute the included flavor packet with sodium-free chicken or beef broth. That's right, just by discarding the included flavor packet and using a sodium-free packet instead, I nor my family have noticed any difference in flavor and I end up cutting almost eighteen hundred milligrams – that's right, 1,800mg of sodium – from a single package of store-bought ramen noodles!

Similar success can be had with almost all seasonings. Just like with making any recipe low-sodium, all you have to do is apply a little 'reverse engineering' to a seasoning recipe in order to figure out how to replicate it. In other words, find out what ingredients your favorite seasoning has in it, and then replace the sodium-based ingredients with sodium-free options. That taco, fajita, or steak seasoning bottle you probably have in your cupboard? I would venture to guess that the nutrition label of every one of them reveals a high level of sodium due to the inclusion of sodium chloride. Furthermore, the serving size that the sodium content is based upon is often very small – probably ¼ tsp or so, much less than you might use on say a pound of ground beef. Therefore, throw them out. Yes, every one of your high-sodium seasonings. Then, spend some quality time making your own – all it takes is a little internet sleuthing.

For example, for fajita night just do an internet search for "fajita seasoning recipe". The first recipe returned in my own search result indicated "chili powder, cumin, paprika, cayenne pepper, garlic powder, salt, and pepper". All you would then have to do for your own great fajita seasoning is develop your own ratio of the same ingredients while utilizing a salt substitute such as potassium chloride for the salt (or foregoing salt altogether). Now, you have a sodium-free option for fajita seasoning to which you can just add some meat, vegetables, and corn tortillas (beware of the sodium content of flour tortillas!) and you have a very-low-sodium meal to enjoy. In a similar fashion, while I used to use a taco meat seasoning packet, my family and I now thrive on just three ingredients for our sodium-free taco meat seasoning: chili powder, garlic, and parsley. I've served it to guests several times and have yet to have one of them ask me what's wrong with the taco meat! Just be sure when working with stock spices to *check every one* for sodium content – many brands of chili powder and other basic spices often include salt. Therefore, I recommend that you only purchase stock spices that do not include salt in the ingredient list.

Speaking of seasonings, recipes based on chicken and beef stock – which are usually loaded with immensely high levels of sodium – are going to be back on your menu as you can now utilize the aforementioned sodium-free stock seasoning. This will open you up to new meal options for soups, stews, seasoned rice, and even some sauces that use stock as a base. Think about it – a nice homemade risotto made from butter, sodium-free chicken stock, Arborio rice, a splash of white wine, and a little parmesan cheese can now be very low-sodium thanks to the sodium-free stock mix. These sodium-free stock mixes can save you hundreds if not thousands of milligrams of sodium per recipe. While these and all low-sodium seasonings may be hard to find in your local grocery store, you will have ample choices to choose from by just going online and finding what you want.

Condiments and snacks

Alongside seasonings, condiments are traditionally high in sodium as well. However, in recent years there have been several types of condiments that have been released with sodium-free or low-sodium options. I've found that some of the biggest traditional offenders such as soy sauce (1000mg or more per serving) now have brands with a true low-sodium option, such as soy sauce with only 145mg per serving. Ketchup, usually loaded with salt in every teaspoon, has a sodium-free option now. With a little luck in the right grocery store (or a quick search on the internet), you'll find salsa and even barbecue sauce with far less than 100mg of sodium per serving, a fraction of the 300-400mg per serving found in the traditional brands. Finding these low-sodium condiments and making adjustments to the respective recipe's ingredients (e.g. corn tortilla vs flour) have allowed me access to low-sodium versions of traditional Chinese and Mexican food and even barbecue options that weren't previously available for me in their traditional form.

Like condiments, you'll find that many of your traditional snacking options are high in sodium but can still be developed into a low-sodium version. For example, I enjoy popcorn several times a week. The microwave version is out due to the high sodium content, but making my own on the stovetop has become a sort of therapy as I know I will soon be enjoying 30 minutes or so of TV time. With a sprinkle of parmesan cheese, some melted unsalted butter, and a little salt substitute (more on that in a minute), I now prefer my skimmed-down version of popcorn to anything that gets made in the microwave. I've also grown fond of unsalted tortilla chips dipped in sour cream or low-sodium salsa, reduced-sodium crackers topped with a piece of Swiss cheese, and lower-sodium versions of granola bars, not to mention the traditional fruit and vegetable snack options as well. It will pay off to invest some time looking for lower-sodium snacking options both in the store and in the kitchen. With smart snacking options you'll create a peace-of-mind for yourself by significantly reducing your intake, you will have more of your sodium budget remaining for your main meals, and you will soon find that you won't be missing the high-sodium counterparts.

Smart choices about meat

A trip through the meat department will reveal that meats are just as vulnerable to the food industry's use of sodium as most other foods. Grab most any packaged meat (say, chicken) and look at the nutrition label. If the sodium content exceeds 100mg per serving, you can bet that the meat has been injected or packaged with a sodium brine solution (it may indicate such on the front of the package). If the meat has been injected with brine, the manufacturer used needles to inject a high-sodium broth into the meat in order to enhance the flavor and in some cases 'plump up' the meat. We're used to this use of a brine injection with pork products like bacon (which now has lower-sodium options as well), but you'll find that it can occur across all meats. Why this matters for you is that a naturally low-sodium meat was saturated with a sodium brine for no real reason other than flavoring. So, when shopping for meats, look for those meats that are fresh and/or not injected with brine.

When it comes to meats like chicken and steaks, I have good success choosing those meats found on the store shelves that are wrapped in cellophane and sitting on Styrofoam trays. These meats may or may not have a nutrition label since they are often cut and packaged in the store. If that happens, the employees are often happy to talk about the quality and preparation of the meat and they can tell you if it was injected or rubbed with salt. Be cautious when shopping for meat, though, as two similarly-packaged meat products such as chicken can be right next to each other in the cooler, with company A's being injected while chicken from company B is not injected. Therefore, be sure to develop a habit of always double-checking the sodium content on the nutrition label (if one is present) which should help prevent you from making the mistake I have made several times by just grabbing a package of meat and throwing it into my cart, only to find out later at home that I grabbed the injected version. Always verify!

Reducing sodium in the preparation of your food

So far we have talked about choosing the best options for your ingredients, specifically how using low-sodium ingredients such as seasoning and meats will set the foundation for a low-sodium meal. Now, we will look at ways to reduce sodium when preparing your own food. Remember from an earlier chapter that sodium bicarbonate or even sodium chloride itself is often a *requirement* of the recipe for items such as breads in order for the recipe to work. Whereas these ingredients are required, there can be consequences if you choose to simply forego adding these ingredients. Yet at other times you will find that you can substitute an ingredient that has less sodium and has no real consequence to your recipe other than a potential reduction in flavor. The rationale behind the addition of sodium to a recipe is important, as it can often influence whether your recipe will be successful.

When adding any sodium-based ingredient to a recipe, you are directly influencing the amount of sodium you are going to consume. Therefore, if at all possible I recommend excluding these products from the recipe if their only purpose is for flavor enhancement. For example, if adding salt to a recipe is simply for taste, salt substitutes should be considered in place of the recipe's salt requirement. Salt substitutes come in a variety of forms ranging from straight potassium chloride to a mixture of potassium chloride and sodium chloride (i.e. salt 'lite'). These seasonings are intended to mimic the taste produced from sodium chloride while either reducing or eliminating sodium chloride itself from the recipe. For many people, salt substitutes improve the flavor of bland foods; however, some people find that the addition of potassium chloride makes the food too bitter. You will have to experiment on your own to determine if the substitutes are worth adding or if it's better to go without. Be aware, though, that individuals who have a sensitivity to potassium may want to first consult with their medical professional before using potassium-based salt substitutes.

When excluding salt from a recipe can influence the outcome of the recipe itself (such as for breads), it is generally recommended that salt substitutes containing reduced levels of sodium be used. The mixture of potassium chloride and sodium chloride still provide enough sodium to exert the necessary effects required by the recipe (e.g. strengthen gluten in the dough). It may take some trial and error to determine the precise amount salt substitute to use in order to ensure that the recipe turns out as planned.

Salting for flavor alone

You will often see a recipe that requires adding an amount of salt "to taste". What this means is that the recipe creator leaves it up to you to add as much salt as you prefer. In other words, the recipe is calling for salt as a matter of improving taste only. If you come across this in a recipe you like, eliminate it – you won't miss it and you'll consume much less sodium than listed in the recipe. One of my biggest pet peeves I see in television or internet recipe preparation shows them lightly seasoning meat or vegetables with salt and pepper right before they pour cups of liquid right over the meat. Skipping that initial addition of salt is not going to affect the flavor of the recipe in any detectable way. In fact, there is most likely sodium in the food already, so it's not likely that you are going to significantly improve the flavor of the dish just by adding a sprinkle of salt!

Let me add a point of emphasis about withholding salt from a recipe. Whereas I generally remove salt from a recipe, I'll typically let my guests know that it's very low in salt and that they will likely want to add salt before they eat it. My palate has adjusted to a reduced sodium intake, but that doesn't mean that everyone else's has. I don't want to 'force' my low-sodium lifestyle on others; rather, I maintain a belief that sodium intake is an issue for me and me only. Therefore, as I don't expect others to limit their intake I will always have a salt shaker around to let others salt their food as necessary.

When you *have* to use a sodium product

Remember from several points made in this book that our bodies require sodium. As a result of our bodies requiring sodium in order to function, it must be understood that your goal is not to be 'sodium free' or eat only sodium-free foods. Quite frankly, Western diets don't make it easy to maintain a sodium-free diet, and there's really no need to try to do so as our bodies do require some sodium. Besides, maintaining a diet without any sodium isn't realistically sustainable over the long term, so it's much more viable to strive for a diet that is low in sodium.

While we have focused so far in this chapter on looking for ingredients that have a low-sodium option, there are going to be times when you might not be able to use the lowest-sodium product. This may be due to a store being sold out of your preferred NSA product, or there just aren't any low-sodium options for your particular food. This happens to me when I buy a bulk amount of frozen seafood such as salad shrimp or fish fillets as well as some types of frozen vegetables (yes, even frozen items can still be coated in salt by some manufacturers). I love fish tacos, and it's more economical to buy a bag of frozen fish fillets than a pound of fresh fish, and doing so ensures that I have plenty of fish left over for future use. However, most frozen seafood – even though it's unseasoned – will typically show 'fish' and 'salt' on the ingredient list along with a relatively high sodium content. Whereas I love my seafood, I buy it regardless of the added salt. Then, I pull out my own kitchen-based version of 'special weapons and tactics' in order to reduce the level of sodium.

As the fish (or vegetables) is frozen, it's going to need to be thawed out before use. Rather than leaving it on the counter, I soak the frozen filets in room temperature water. Given that the seafood is coated in salt, I use a special kind of water – deionized. Why? Deionized water has effectively no sodium ions present. And, if you think back to Chapter 2 you'll remember our discussion about a concentration gradient, right? Since the deionized water has no sodium present, diffusion will pull the sodium ions off of the fish and into the water.

Would tap water work – absolutely! In fact, an old study from 1984 found that there was no difference in the amount of sodium removed from packaged food after soaking and rinsing in either deionized or tap water [2]. However, the study also mentioned that the sodium content of tap water is highly variable. So, I looked into what my area's tap water sodium concentration was and found out that it was 100mg per liter – one of the highest concentrations of all cities on the list! Since diffusion will remove sodium up to the point that it equals the concentration of the water it is being soaked in, I feel better starting with water that has effectively no sodium present, as it will remove more sodium from the food. Given that I pay less than $1.00 for a gallon of deionized water, the peace-of-mind is welcome for such a minimum investment.

I can't always use a deionized soak, such as when we're cooking out in the country and a grocery store isn't available. In such cases, when I need an emergency use of something like canned vegetables and a low-sodium version isn't available, a simple washing with tap water is a quick way to remove a significant amount of sodium. The vast majority of sodium is found in the liquid brine, so dumping off the brine and rinsing the actual food product will serve to remove a good amount of sodium. Granted, some sodium will remain within the food product itself and therefore be unaffected by a simple rinse, so if you're concerned about that 'unwashable' sodium affecting your sodium budget, you may want to consider the deionized water soak.

A final thought about home-cooked meals

Preparing your own food can be quite enjoyable and brings you peace of mind in knowing exactly how much sodium is in your food. To make it easier on yourself, get into the mindset that you are going to strive to focus your diet on low-sodium or sodium-free foods. Therefore, build your meals around ingredients that are naturally low-sodium such as rice, pasta, ground beef, and non-injected chicken, as these are all great food frameworks around which to base a meal (but always double-check the nutrition label!). By using a low-sodium base ingredient such as rice or pasta, you allow yourself more wiggle room in your budget that might allow you to have a higher-sodium item such as a glaze or sauce.

As we've talked about how to reduce sodium through quality ingredients and smart choices in food preparation, it goes without saying that when enjoying your food, avoid the salt shaker at the dinner table. Even though only about 10% of our daily sodium intake comes from sodium added after the food has been prepared, eliminating the shaker will cut down significantly on your daily intake if you have previously been gratuitously salting your food when it's on your plate. If you previously added salt at the table to a large enough degree, expect to cut out 500mg of sodium or more from your daily intake just by removing the salt shaker, a major improvement if you're intending to go low-sodium.

Staying low-sodium when eating out

We discussed earlier how eating and preparing your own meals at home provides a lot of control regarding what goes into your food. Dining out removes a lot of that control as you are not directly involved in the food preparation and therefore you can't be certain about what goes into your meal. Fast food and restaurant food ordered straight from the menu are effectively out when on a low-sodium diet, as the sodium levels can be astronomical. However, you can still enjoy trips to your favorite restaurants if the food can be prepared properly. While cooking low-sodium food in your own kitchen was all about adding the right ingredients, dining out is more about making the right food choices when you order. Though you might have to give up a favorite restaurant dish if the sodium can't be reduced, rest assured that you can still enjoy the fun and convenience of restaurant food.

One of the best things you can do before going out to eat is making sure that you set yourself up for success. First, understand that certain cuisines are going to be higher in sodium than others. Asian, Italian, and barbecue restaurants use ample amounts of sauces that typically contain a high level of sodium. Seafood restaurants, for example, will typically include sodium-heavy dry seasoning sprinkled on the fish or seafood. Therefore, do your best to find restaurants that serve fresh ingredients – especially in the way of meats, vegetables, and fruits. A small dinner with a low-sodium dessert will likely provide you a fun night out and still keep you well within your sodium budget. However, your likelihood of having 'fun' is largely dependent upon you recognizing that your old way of eating out doesn't exist anymore. In turn, you have to adjust to your new low-sodium lifestyle rather than expecting it to adjust to you.

Another thing to help ensure an enjoyable dining experience is to make sure you are a well-informed customer. Select your restaurant before you leave your house, and once you pick your restaurant, get on the internet and pull up the restaurant's nutrition guide. Most all of the chain restaurants have their nutritional information on their website (though I often have better luck just searching for the name of the restaurant and the words 'nutrition information'). Once you know the menu's sodium-heavy foods you can get an idea of which type of menu items to avoid. If you have a particular dish in mind that you'd like to eat, feel free to call the restaurant and ask if there is a low-sodium way to prepare the dish. A phone call lets the restaurant know that getting your business is on the line, and you will find that they will often present several options to you to earn your business.

This brings up another point that can help you enjoy eating out. Even though a restaurant's nutrition menu shows a high amount of sodium, in many cases you'll find that the vast majority of that sodium comes from seasoning. Take the aforementioned seafood restaurant. If the fish is cut fresh at the restaurant (meaning it's not shipped frozen and packed in a sodium brine), the only real option for having high sodium in the dish is if it is coated in seasoning, as it often is. Therefore, you will likely have many additional options if you order your food unseasoned. Beware though, that the waiter does not often know if the food is truly 'fresh'. Therefore, ask if they cut their own fries, make their own burger patties, or even cut their own steaks. If they do, you can expect that the restaurant will be able to serve you a plain meal, to which you can add your own seasoning – including that which you bring yourself. If the food is cooked from frozen patties or bagged fries, for example, expect that they are already seasoned. If you're not sure, ask to verify! I remember one situation where I ordered a hamburger and I asked them to not add any salt. "We don't salt our burgers" was their reply. I asked if they made their burgers with fresh meat, and they said no, but they did use frozen patties from a bag. Because I had a friendly relationship with the person cooking the food, I asked if I could just see the bag in which the patties were packed. Wouldn't you know, the pre-seasoned burger patties were loaded with 800mg of sodium! Because of situations like this, I have told many waiters that I would like my food unseasoned, and if it is served with – or comes already loaded with - seasoning, I will send it back. Ask nicely and it will be clear that you're not coming off as rude. Personally, I've always had waiters that are happy to find out. And for their extra effort, I'm always willing to tip graciously!

When placing your order, I recommend that you make it clear that you want it prepared without *seasoning*. You might think I mean 'without salt', but so many seasonings include salt that it's likely that withholding just salt would have no real effect against the other salt-containing seasonings (such as Cajun spice, fajita seasonings, or chili powder). Some restaurants consider this type of food as being ordered "plain", but I prefer to be more specific and state that the food needs to be prepared with no seasoning added at all. I may even emphasize my point by telling the waiter that I have a reaction if I consume to too much salt (which is true). If you called the restaurant previously to ask about making a dish low-sodium, let the waiter know that you talked to a particular person. Remember, the waiter is not going to be a low-sodium aficionado, so they won't be as in-tune with the logistics of low-sodium as you will. But, I think you'll find that they'll almost always work with you or find someone who can, as they all want you to be able to enjoy your time dining out. For me, the more confident I am that my food is prepared properly, the more I can enjoy my meal when eating out such as when I partake in one of my favorite restaurant dishes – an unseasoned steak cooked rare with a side of unsalted French fries. When cooked right, the true taste of the steak is evident, much more so than when I had previously sprinkled on ample amounts of salt.

I've rarely had a restaurant say that they cannot accommodate me in making an un-seasoned dish (remember, you are typically in control here as they want to ensure that you enjoy your experience). If they do state that they can't serve the dish, it's likely because the food is already pre-seasoned, such as a frozen patty or filet coated with seasoning. In many cases, you'll find that certain restaurant items are made in bulk and therefore you won't have a low-sodium option for that particular food. In those cases, such as might occur with pasta sauce or a salad dressing, request the sauce or dressing on the side. I've spent many dinners lightly dipping plain pasta into sauce, and I take a good deal of satisfaction in seeing quite a bit of sauce remaining once my pasta is gone. You'll also likely find out over time that your food has a delicious natural taste, one that you might even prefer more than when it was coated in sauce.

A final option that has worked well for me is to consider a restaurant that has a salad bar option. If I arrive at the restaurant and don't feel confident about the sodium options, I have no problem ordering a salad bar plate as I am confident that the fresh ingredients will result in a meal that is well below my sodium budget. Those restaurants with a full salad bar are always more favorable for me than ordering a salad off of the menu as I will rarely get 'full' off of one salad. The salad bar option, on the other hand, allows me to make multiple trips until I'm full. However, if a restaurant without a salad bar is chosen and I feel more confident about my sodium options by ordering just a salad, a nice dessert will often make up the difference if the salad doesn't fill me up. Remember – dining out on a low-sodium lifestyle will take a few adjustments on your part but you will learn to embrace the lifestyle, and you will soon discover that dining out can still be an enjoyable experience for you as well as those you are with.

Staying low-sodium in social gatherings

The last setting we need to look at is that of the social gathering, as it can present unique challenges to a low-sodium lifestyle. You might be asking 'what exactly qualifies as a social gathering setting?'. I don't know the formal definition, but I like to think of social gatherings as the football game tailgates and watch parties, the holiday get-togethers with friends, or maybe a family reunion. These settings aren't quite the formal dining-out experience, but at the same time you're not exactly in control of the food even though it's home-cooked. If the gathering is a festive atmosphere centered around something like a football or basketball game, you can bet that the food will mostly consist of high-sodium appetizers and other snack foods rather than the entrees that are more likely to be found at longer gatherings like reunions or holiday events. Despite some unique challenges when it comes to sticking to your low-sodium diet at these social gathering events, it's still easy to enjoy the time as well as the food.

If the event is a 'pot luck' style gathering where everyone is expected to bring a dish, I have no worries about watching my sodium as I can simply bring my own dish and spend my time snacking on that. Regardless of whether it asks for appetizers or entrées, I have plenty of low-sodium option available. I have no qualms about bringing sodium-free tortilla chips and a simple dip. If the event calls for an entrée, I usually stick with a party-style dish such as crock-pot meatballs or a pasta salad. When the time to eat rolls around I won't give a second-thought about eating mostly from the dish that I brought. Similar to the goal of dining out, enjoying social gatherings is about being comfortable with what I'm eating.

There are going to be those times when you have to attend an office party, kid's birthday, or other event where there won't be much of any low-sodium options that you can feel confident about. I've had this happen many times where the main offering was going to be chicken wings or maybe pizza. In these types of situations I usually go one of two ways. If there are no dishes like a fruit or vegetable tray offered, I will likely just bear down and avoid eating at all. If this is a possibility and I know beforehand that it might occur, I will often employ my second option and eat before I get to the event. I'd rather be full before arriving and not be tempted to have just one slice or piece of a high-sodium food than to suffer the potential consequences of eating more than I should and triggering a Ménière's episode.

I can't remember a single time that I've ever been chastised for not eating food at a kid's birthday party. Most of my friends and co-workers are aware of my low-sodium diet, so there isn't much issue when I politely decline a food option. Other times, though, I'm offered something like a piece of pizza and end up having to decline, either with or (hopefully) without a brief discussion of my diet. Some prior effort on your part – such as a casual conversation with your co-workers in the weeks leading up to a holiday or party event outlining how you're on a low-sodium diet – can often prevent those awkward long talks that will occur when someone says "surely you can have one piece of pizza, right?". You'll find out that in the end pretty much everyone is going to be receptive to your situation, even though they just might not quite understand it at first. And if you're like me you'll find that even though you have a unique dietary situation, you'll be treated just like any other individual.

References

1. Rauch, S. D. (2010). "Clinical Hints and Precipitating Factors in Patients Suffering from Meniere's Disease." <u>Otolaryngologic Clinics of North America</u> **43**(5): 1011-1017.

2. Weaver, C. M., et al. (1984). "Removal of electrolytes from institutionally packaged foods." <u>Journal of the American Dietetic Association</u> **84**(3): 319-322.

Chapter 8: Living the low-sodium lifestyle

Having made it to this point in the book, consider yourself armed and dangerous. When it comes to sodium, this book was designed to provide you the essential information necessary to make you not only a healthier and more knowledgeable individual but also a more savvy consumer. If you're like me, you'll now exhibit a heightened awareness about the food world around you. You won't associate foods with cost or even taste as much as you will sodium content. In fact, because of its prevalence in our foods, your whole association with food will probably begin to revolve around sodium!

It is important to understand that when it comes to sodium intake there is a difference between engaging in a low-sodium lifestyle for your own health versus a medical necessity. For someone like myself it is critical that I stay on a low-sodium diet for medical reasons. Others – perhaps even you – may choose a low-sodium lifestyle for health reasons, meaning that you are aware of the effects of consuming excess sodium and want to avoid those effects even if there is not a specific or immediate consequence of consuming too much sodium. For some of you, the low-sodium lifestyle may not work out. If you are going low-sodium by choice, you can simply revert back to your old diet. However, if low-sodium is recommended to you or a loved one due to a medical condition, be sure to consult with your healthcare professional before going back to your old diet.

For those of you that want to continue on with your low-sodium lifestyle, no matter your reason for pressing onward, remember that it is *your* choice and *your* lifestyle. You will find that going low-sodium can go so far as to influence your social groups in the same way that social support can help someone trying to lose weight. For me, my friends know that I am very picky about my food because of my sodium choices. Every once in a while someone will ask why, and I'm happy to inform them. But I am also mindful of the fact that no one else around me is sodium-conscious; therefore I don't expect everyone else to adhere to – or even agree with – my low-sodium lifestyle.

Everyone has their own little quirk in life. Mine is low-sodium, and others have theirs. If you find that you are in a situation whereby you are constantly criticized or questioned, you may want to reconsider your social circle. Granted, low-sodium has not received the recent publicity of other health issues such as gluten-free or ketogenic diets and as such your friends may not understand your rationale, but again, it is your choice and you deserve the respect of those around you. Think about it this way – would your social criticize a recovering alcoholic friend of yours if he or she did not want to attend a gathering at a cocktail bar? Or, would they be respectful of his or her condition and understand their reasoning? If you think they'd avoid any criticizing of the recovering alcoholic, why would they not consider and be respectful of your low-sodium situation as well?

I've learned that you'll get a better response by being a passive educator than being a low-sodium activist. In other words, when someone asks me why I can't have sodium I'll tell them. But, I never chastise or complain about someone else's high-sodium food choices. I've learned that if you are accepting and respectful of the group – meaning that you aren't demanding a low-sodium eating establishment every time but rather just a place that offers *you* options such as a salad bar – then the group will be more accommodating in finding an eating establishment that everyone can enjoy.

Understand that this mindset of applying your low-sodium lifestyle applies to your home life, also. As we have discussed, you have much less control of sodium at a restaurant than you will have at home. So while eating at home provides a wealth of food options that you may not be able to enjoy at a restaurant, remember also that salt is a flavor enhancer and most people have grown accustomed to the flavors that salt provides. Therefore, if you undertake the low-sodium lifestyle at home you will have to walk the fine line of cooking low sodium meals but also maintaining sanity within your household. If you have a spouse and/or kids in the home, they have likely been used to eating regular (i.e. high-sodium) foods without consequence. If you thrust a low-sodium lifestyle on them too quickly they may revolt! In my own household I am conscious of this, as our pantry is full of foods that run the full range of sodium content – from seasoned potato chips to a variety of no-salt-added vegetables. I have no problem with my kids eating some nacho-cheese-flavored tortilla chips for a snack, as those opportunities get balanced out with other meals that include carrots or fruit in addition to the low-sodium options that I cook. And, I have been blessed with a wife who has never once complained of or told me she was tired of the low-sodium meals we eat. I like to think that this is due to an effort to cook meals that are flavorful but still low in sodium. And because of the success I have had over the years in developing recipes into my own low-sodium version, I hope that you have the same opportunity.

Conclusion

So there you have it – your introduction to the world of sodium and the lifestyle of being low-sodium. I hope that this book has opened your eyes to what sodium is and has helped you grasp both the relative complexity and the immense benefits of living a low-sodium lifestyle. I know that when I started on this path I didn't have one good, solid reference to help me understand the why, the what, and the how when it came to being smart about sodium. That lack of a reference is what drove me to write this book. I hope that my own trials, successes, and failures can help you live a more enjoyable life, and I also hope that you see that maintaining a low-sodium diet is not an obstacle but rather a different pathway. I can tell you that in having a medical condition myself that is affected by sodium, the benefits of staying low-sodium far outweigh any inconveniences. And, the improvement in my quality of life that being low-sodium brings me fully justifies the minimal additional effort I need to put into adhering to the lifestyle.

One of my goals for this book is that no matter your own reason for embarking on a low-sodium lifestyle, you have learned valuable information in this book that will make your efforts more meaningful as well as more successful. If you're like me, sodium will soon become a way of life when it comes to your food. You will likely begin to pay less attention to price and more attention to the Nutrition Facts label. You'll become creative in finding ways to eat foods that you *want* to eat while still controlling your sodium intake. And maybe you'll even find that foods taste better when they're not first bathed in sodium.

In closing, let's talk about my vision for this lifestyle. In my mind, there is simply no physiological need to consume the high amounts of sodium that we as a society do. Yes, sodium plays a role in food preservation, and it certainly makes food taste better. But my belief remains that we don't *need* to consume high sodium, we just "do it" anyway. My arguments are based on the evidence. While sodium is important to food preservation, no-salt-added canned foods have an identical shelf life (as indicated by the 'best before' or expiration date) as their high-sodium cousins despite having 1/10th or less of sodium content. This indicates that the traditional, high-sodium brines inherent to many foods just isn't necessary for preservation. And as for taste, would consumers really notice if half the salt was added to a restaurant dish? Are soups *that* unpalatable with 200mg of sodium per serving as opposed to 1200mg? These are not questions I intend to solve; rather, they're just a couple of those "things that make you go hmmm".

For me, I'll feel a small sense of pride in seeing low-sodium options become more prevalent, similar to the growth of gluten-free foods appearing with more frequency in grocery stores and on restaurant menus. If we can advance the low-sodium lifestyle in the food industry I think that the effects will be not only improved health for all, but I think we can also generate lower overall medical costs. And when medical costs are influenced, the government usually tends to take notice. But government-induced change ultimately occurs only after years of research and millions of dollars in funding. Even though there is ongoing research touting the benefits of decreasing our sodium intake, the effects I would love to see just aren't catching on yet. Until then, it may be just you and me on this journey. Unless of course, you can influence those around you as well.

I wish you the best of luck on your journey with low sodium!

Appendix - Recipes

I don't think that this book would be complete without at least a couple of low-sodium recipes. Though I never set out to develop this book as an actual recipe book, I have over time realized that I have too many low-sodium recipes that I have worked out over time to *not* make a recipe book eventually. I have found a wealth of recipes that seem intent on copying an existing recipe and just switching out any addition of salt with a salt substitute. But as I have outlined in this book, sodium exists in many ingredients other than just salt. Or, the dish is so small that there is no real adjustment needed in sodium since you'll be taking in so little food anyway.

Taking note of these aspects, I have spent a lot of time developing my own recipes that both myself and my family enjoy. This includes entrées, soups, and desserts alike, among others. So in this last section, I'll leave you a few of my favorites for you to enjoy. These recipes outline the *total* sodium content of the prepared dish using low-sodium ingredients I have found, so adjust as necessary if you eat less than the whole dish! Sorry I don't have any pictures for you to enjoy, but I thought that you'd much rather see the sodium content and enjoy the food than have a professionally-photographed food item. Besides, I need to save at least *something* for the recipe book, right?

Spaghetti

Ingredients (total sodium content in mg):

- *1/3 pound ground beef (100)*
- *1 tsp olive oil (0)*
- *½ yellow onion, diced (10)*
- *½ green pepper diced (5)*
- *2 cans (14.5 oz), no-salt-added petite-diced tomatoes (100)*
- *1 can (8 oz) no-salt-added tomato sauce (70)*
- *½ tsp garlic powder (0)*
- *1 tbsp finely chopped basil (0)*
- *1 tsp oregano (0)*
- *½ tsp black pepper (0)*
- *16 oz spaghetti (0)*

Total ingredient sodium: 285mg

Directions

In a skillet, sauté the onion and green pepper in the olive oil until soft (approximately 5 minutes). Remove from the pan and then brown the ground beef. Once brown, add the onions and peppers back in, along with the diced tomatoes, tomato sauce, garlic, basil, oregano, and black pepper and heat to a boil, then reducing to a simmer for ten minutes. While simmering, cook the spaghetti per package directions, and then drain.

Plate a large helping of spaghetti and then add the meat sauce over the top.

Nachos Grande

Ingredients (total sodium content in mg):

- *½ pound of ground beef (150)*
- *¾ cup water (0)*
- *1 tsp parsley (0)*
- *1 tsp NSA chili powder (0)*
- *½ tsp garlic powder (0)*
- *½ bag of unsalted tortilla chips, crushed (50)*
- *¼ cup shredded cheddar cheese (200)*
- *½ cup diced yellow onion (5)*
- *1 cup diced roma tomato (0)*
- *3 cups diced iceberg lettuce (0)*
- *5 tbsp sour cream (50)*
- *5 tbsp homemade salsa (100)*

Total ingredient sodium: 555mg

Directions

Brown the ground beef. When browned, add the water, chili powder, garlic powder, and parsley. Simmer on medium until most of the water has cooked off. Once the meat is ready, place an ample base of chips on a plate, followed by a spoonful of meat, then cheese, onions, tomato, and lettuce. Top with sour cream and salsa, and enjoy!.

Green-beaned meat over rice

Ingredients (total sodium content in mg):

- *1lb ground beef (300)*
- *1 medium onion, chopped (20)*
- *½ tsp garlic powder (0)*
- *1 ½ cups water (0)*
- *3 tbsp low sodium soy sauce (435)*
- *1 tbsp dark molasses (0)*
- *1 can NSA French style or cut green beans, drained (70)*
- *1 tbsp cornstarch (0)*
- *1/4cup cold water (0)*

Total ingredient sodium: 825mg

Directions

Brown the ground beef with the chopped onion. Once browned, add the garlic powder, water, low-sodium soy sauce, and molasses, and bring to a boil. Add the green beans. While cooking, prepare the rice. One minute before serving, dissolve the cornstarch in the ¼ cup of water and then stir the mixture into the meat preparation. Serve a spoonful of the meat mixture over a helping of rice.

Classic meatballs

Ingredients (total sodium content in mg)

- *1 tsp olive oil (0)*
- *1 large onion finely diced (30)*
- *½ tsp garlic powder (0)*
- *1.5 pounds ground beef (450)*
- *1 large egg (75)*
- *1/4 cup grated parmesan cheese (200)*
- *2 tbsp parsley (0)*
- *1 cup unseasoned breadcrumbs (100)*
- *1 tsp salt substitute (0)*
- *1/2 cup water (0)*

Total ingredient sodium: 855mg

Directions

Preheat the oven to 350 degrees F. In a large oven-safe skillet, add the olive oil and onions and cook over medium heat until the onions become translucent. meanwhile, in a bowl add the remaining ingredients and mix with your hands. Add the cooked onions and give one final mix. Then, form the mixture into individual balls of your preferred side and add them to the skillet. One all meatballs have been added to the skillet, cook the meatballs for 2-3 minutes on top and bottom, then transfer the skillet to the oven and cook for an additional 15-20 minutes (time depends upon the size of your meatballs).

Chicken Noodle Soup

Ingredients (total sodium content in mg)

- 1 pound of chicken breast (120)
- 6 cups of water (0)
- 4 tsp NSA chicken broth powder (0)
- ¼ cup, carrot shavings (10)
- 1 tsp basil (0)
- ½ tsp garlic powder (0)
- ½ tsp crushed black pepper (0)
- ½ stalk celery, diced (30)
- ½ yellow onion, diced (5)
- 1 16-oz box of rotini noodles (0)

Total ingredient sodium: 165mg

Directions

In a small skillet, add ¼ cup of water and chicken breast. Cover and cook on medium until done, then shred. Add 6 cups of water to a soup pot and bring to boil. To the boiling water add NSA chicken broth, basil, garlic powder, black pepper, and diced celery, and diced carrot. Add the shredded chicken to the soup pot and reduce the heat to medium-low. While that pot is simmering, cook the rotini per package directions, drain, and then add to the soup pot. Simmer for five minutes before serving

Other published books written by Mark Knoblauch

In addition to *Surviving Low Sodium*, Mark has released several other books and is also working on several more. And, if you are interested in academic writing, be sure to check out his academic textbook entitled *Professional Writing in Kinesiology and Sports Medicine*.

Overcoming Ménière's. How changing your lifestyle can change your life.

ISBN# 978-1-7320674-7-9

Overcoming Ménière's provides the reader a detailed overview of Ménière's including the involved anatomy along with the most recent research. By detailing his own Ménière's journey as well as what has worked for his own battle with Ménière's, Mark intends to provide other Ménière's sufferers a pathway which they themselves can following in order to find similar relief from the devastating effects of Ménière's disease.

Understanding BPPV. Outlining the causes and effects of Benign Paroxysmal Positional Vertigo

ISBN# 978-1-7320674-1-7

Benign Paroxysmal Positional Vertigo is a condition that triggers vertigo when the head is placed in a particular position. Furthermore, the vertigo ceases once the head is repositioned. Despite the somewhat forceful symptoms inherent to BPPV, the underlying cause of BPPV is relatively minor and can typically be fixed with a simple visit to a medical professional's office.

Because of his own experience with BPPV, Mark wrote *Understanding BPPV* so that everyone affected by this condition can have a solid resource guide outlining just what BPPV is, how it occurs, and how it is treated. Particular attention is focused on the anatomy of the ear, and how this anatomy is involved in generating the symptoms associated with BPPV. Mark also details the latest research into BPPV and provides an overview of the various diagnostic tests and treatments used to help BPPV patients in many cases get back to a vertigo-free life.

Essentials of Writing and Publishing your Self-Help Book

ISBN# 978-1-7320674-9-3

Some people elect to transform their own experiences and successes into a self-help book that outlines how they persevered through their difficult times. As a potential self-help book author yourself, you might be struggling to get started, get finished, or just need tips on how to finally get your advice and ideas onto bookstore shelves. *Essentials of Writing and Publishing Your Self-Help Book* is filled with information that will help walk you through the process of producing a quality self-help book. You'll be exposed to strategies that will help get you through the various stages of book production, gain insight into the options you have available for publication of your book, and review the individual steps and requirements necessary to get your advice from paper to a finished book.

Hidden down deep inside of us, we all have a book waiting to be written. The tips and techniques outlined in this book are designed to help you bring your ideas, successes, and lessons to life in the form of your own self-help book.

Outlining Tinnitus. A comprehensive guide to help you break free of the ringing in your ears.

ISBN: 978-1-7320674-2-4

The underlying cause of tinnitus has been described by researchers as one of the most controversial issues in medical science. Despite decades of intense research, the cure for tinnitus remains elusive. Consequently, millions of tinnitus sufferers are left susceptible to the frustration brought about by the ever-present ringing in their ears. Mark Knoblauch has himself lived with tinnitus for over 15 years and understands the daily battles that occur in those individuals afflicted with tinnitus.

Now, despite still living with tinnitus daily, the high-pitched sound in his ear has become nothing more than an afterthought thanks to a dedicated treatment plan. And the success he had in addressing his own tinnitus drove him to write Outlining Tinnitus. This book is designed to serve as an all-inclusive guide for those individuals who either suffer from tinnitus or those who live with or know someone suffering. Topics such as the involved anatomy, suspected causes, available therapies and treatments, and effects on quality of life are all discussed along with many others in order to provide an overview of what tinnitus is as well as how it can be effectively eliminated.

The art of efficiency. A guide for improving task management in the home to help maximize your leisure time (ebook only)

In a world that seemingly never has enough time, we are often unable to get everything done that we need to accomplish in a given time frame. Though we can take out our frustrations on the fact that there is just not enough time in our day, no matter what we want, we can't simply create more time. Therefore, we have to make the most of the time we do have and try to utilize our available time in the most efficient way possible.

When it comes to getting tasks done in the home, efficiency can be the key to determining how much free time we ultimately earn for ourselves. As we become more efficient, we can expect an improvement in the amount of time available for us to use as we please. This book highlights those tactics that I have found beneficial at helping me get my required tasks done at home in the most efficient way possible. More importantly, this book will show you how to structure your tasks based upon the required activity level (i.e. active vs. passive tasks), in turn being able to schedule your time-on-task in a way that results in significant time savings due to your improved efficiency at task completion.

7 Ways to Make Running Not Suck

ISBN: 978-1-7320674-0-0

Let's face it – running sucks. Those pictures of runners that we see in advertisements showing a smiling, energetic runner in no way represent the agonizing, sweat-covered dread that so many of us put ourselves through in order to stay healthy. Given the vast amount of benefits associated with running, why can't it be more enjoyable?

What if you were told that running does not have to induce misery and can in fact be quite pleasant no matter your fitness level? You've read through the training books and learned how to adjust your nutrition, but what about the other issues that can affect your run? By accounting for several key factors involved with your run such as weather and equipment, you can minimize the opportunity for these same factors to have a negative impact on your run. This can in turn improve your running experience and can also influence your motivation to keep running.

Seven Ways outlines how to account for those ancillary factors that can directly influence the quality of your runs. Based on his own experience as well as information gained from dozens of conversations with both new and experienced runners, Mark Knoblauch guides you through preparing and adapting to these factors as well as how to use them to your advantage.

By reducing the opportunity for negative influences to impact your running, it should be expected that your runs will become more enjoyable and more motivating, which in turn can have a significant impact on both your performance as well as your overall health.

Challenge the Hand You Were Dealt

ISBN: 978-1-7320674-3-1

We all experience some degree of misfortune in our life, and it can often occur without reason or explanation. When there's no real justification as to why we experience adversity, our situation is often explained as being a result of the hand we were dealt. While some might feel a sense of relief in response to the idea that a greater force is actually in control of their circumstances, others refuse to accept this notion and instead choose to confront their situation head-on. Those individuals have chosen to challenge the hand they were dealt.

Mark Knoblauch has long been a challenger. From humble beginnings and through a debilitating disease, he has experienced his share of adversity. With each adverse encounter he faces, he has developed a mindset that allows him to see an obstacle rather than a roadblock. Mark wrote *Challenge the Hand You Were Dealt* based on his philosophy for moving on after experiencing hard times. In this book, Mark outlines how to identify your value and your passions, as well as a variety of techniques for giving yourself the best chance to be successful. Challenge the Hand You Were Dealt was developed with the intent of empowering and motivating you to move past your hardships and to find ways to recognize your own potential for success.

Let others know!

If you found this or any of Mark's other books informative, *please take the time and post a review online*! Reviews help get exposure for the books and thereby improve the chances that others will be able to benefit from the material as well!

Image Credits

About the Author

Since being diagnosed with Ménière's disease in 2011, Mark Knoblauch has remained on a strict low-sodium diet ever since. The success he has had since going low-sodium pushed him to learn more about sodium and its effects on our body, culminating with his writing of this, his tenth book, *Living Low Sodium.*

Mark is a small-town Kansas native who now lives in a suburb of Houston with his wife and two young daughters. His background is in the area of sports medicine, obtaining his bachelor's degree from Wichita State and his master's degree from the University of Nevada, Las Vegas. After working clinically as an athletic trainer for eight years, Mark returned to graduate school where he received his doctorate in Kinesiology from the University of Houston, followed by a postdoctoral assistantship in Molecular Physiology and Biophysics at Baylor College of Medicine in Houston, TX. He has been employed as a college professor at the University of Houston since 2013.